بِسْمِ اللهِ الرَّحْمَنِ الرَّحِيمِ

Cover calligraphy: Aisha Wright

Lifeboat Press

Contact: abdussabur.kirke@gmail.com

ISBN: 978-0-6397-0737-2
Manufactured in the United Kingdom

KHUTBAS

Abdussabur Kirke

LIFEBOAT PRESS

CONTENTS

Islam is not a Concept

Allah, tabaraka wa ta'ala, says in Surat al-Muminun:

$$\text{فَتَعَـٰلَى ٱللَّهُ ٱلْمَلِكُ ٱلْحَقُّ لَآ إِلَـٰهَ إِلَّا هُوَ رَبُّ ٱلْعَرْشِ ٱلْكَرِيمِ ۝}$$

Exalted be Allah,
the King, the Real.
There is no god but Him,
Lord of the Noble Throne.

The one to whom Muslims bow down is not 'a god'.
They do not bow to an entity. They do not bow to an
idea. They do not bow to the 'Islamic concept' of god.
The one to whom Muslims submit is not 'their' god

as opposed to the god of other religions. There can be only one Reality. Muslims do not own that Reality. It is not for man to define Reality, except with that by which it has defined itself. We submit to Reality, but it is not made real by virtue of us or our submission. Reality does not require our submission, but we have to submit. Reality has defined itself and named itself. Allah is the name that Reality has given itself. He, may He be glorified, is the Real: al-Haqq.

He is not a concept. He has no gender. Neither Muslims nor their Prophet have conceived Him; rather He has conceived them and us, but not in the sense of giving birth. He is not a thing. He is the originator of things. He is not the 'greatest of all things'. He is greater – 'akbar' – in the sense that all greatness in this world is but an indication of His absolute greatness. Limits are for the world. He is the setter of limits and He is not subject to limitation. Our knowing Him or not knowing Him does not change Him. But it changes us.

Islam is not a concept and there are no such thing as Islamic concepts. Concepts are born in the minds of men. Islamic concepts are a departure from the Real and a departure from the knowledge of the first community of Muslims and the imprinting they received from the Messenger by being in his presence, may Allah bless him and grant him peace. The transaction of the

Muslim is submission to the Real and acceptance of the Messenger. When Muslims bow down, they bow down to Reality. They do not bow down to 'their god'. The Real sent His Prophet Muhammad, may Allah bless him and grant him peace, whom He created without fault and whom He made truthful and obedient to Him – and what could be easier for Allah than to make someone in whatever way He wishes? Who is man to doubt, based on his own ignorance, the light which Allah has given to His Prophets and anyone else He wishes?

The Prophet Muhammad, may Allah bless him and grant him peace, was sent to show people how to submit to Reality, and so to be in harmony with themselves and their Lord and in appropriate relations with all of creation.

The Muslim has realised his own evanescence in the face of Allah's absolute permanence. He has recognised the Prophet Muhammad, may Allah bless him and grant him peace, as the perfect exemplar in character and in submission to the Real – the perfect slave of Allah. The Muslims say, the *perfected* slave of Allah, because his perfection was from Allah, not by his own achievement, may Allah bless him and grant him peace, although he did also demonstrate every good quality that can be attained by human achievement, and he achieved them all. Emulation of the Messenger is the road the Muslim takes towards perfecting his own submission and obedience to Reality, and his own good character and nature, although he can never attain to the Messenger's station, may Allah bless him and grant him peace. Rather we hope that Allah covers our qualities with His Qualities and we hope to be blessed with even just a portion of the Light of Muhammad, may Allah bless him and grant him peace.

The Muslim has accepted the sublime and overwhelming event of Revelation: the descent of the Word of Allah into the heart of the Messenger, may Allah bless him and grant him peace. It descends not in the spatial sense but from the higher realm to the tongue of creation. The Word of Allah exists outside of time and place. It descends into the realm of time and space as the recited words of Qur'an, which were delivered by the Messenger, the Prophet Muhammad, to his Companions, who memorised it and wrote it down. It is that which we recite.

Allah says in His Noble Book:

$$\text{فَٱقۡرَءُواْ مَا تَيَسَّرَ مِنَ ٱلۡقُرۡءَانِ}$$

Recite as much of the Qur'an as is easy for you.

Submission to the Real does not imply submissiveness

in the world. He who fears his Lord, does not fear creation. Submission to the Real means balance, sanity, compassion, equanimity, generosity, wisdom, tact, excellence, strength, courage and every other good quality, all of which were exemplified by the Messenger of Allah, Muhammad, may Allah bless him and grant him peace, because of his perfect and uninterrupted slavehood and perfected character. Any shortage of these qualities is due to the particular inadequacies of each person, to which every human is subject, with the exception of the Prophets and Messengers. Only the Prophets and Messengers such as Adam, Ibrahim, 'Isa, Musa and Muhammad, may Allah grant peace to all of them, are free of fault – because they were created as clean vessels for His guidance and Revelation. We are flawed, but we do not dwell on our flaws or indulge in guilt. We dwell on the greatness and Mercy of our Lord and the perfect and beautiful qualities of our Messenger, may Allah bless him and grant him peace, and all the Prophets and Messengers, and we have a good opinion of the Muslims, refrain from bad opinion and make seventy excuses for our brothers and sisters in the Deen.

Nothing that can be said about Islam can hit the mark without acknowledging Allah's absolute perfection and absolute singularity and His power, which is unconditional. Conditionality does not reach Him. His hands are not tied. There is not a leaf that falls without His permission.

Al-An'am (60):

وَمَا تَسْقُطُ مِنْ وَرَقَةٍ اِلَّا يَعْلَمُهَا

No leaf falls without His knowing it.

The one who witnesses His perfection, singularity and power understands and is safe in the created world, which is the world of imperfection and multiplicity, because he has turned away from his own imperfection and multiplicity and is looking at the perfection and singularity of His Lord.

Nothing that can be said about Islam can hit the mark without acknowledging the perfect station of the Messenger, recognition of which is recognition of one's own Adamic core and potential for integrity. Recognising his perfection is an act of self-trust, since it reflects a recognition of our own real nature – the nature which knows and is at home in true slavehood.

* * *

Allah, subhanahu wa ta'ala, says in Surat al-Baqara:

$$\text{وَأَحَلَّ اللَّهُ الْبَيْعَ وَحَرَّمَ الرِّبَوا}$$

Allah has permitted trade and He has forbidden riba.

Islam's prohibition of riba is the most important message for our particular time. Beside it, all other social and political issues pale. Without hearing it and obeying it, humankind will continue its present descent, of which current social and financial experiments are but an acceleration.

What is riba? Riba is an unjustified, unnatural increase in a transaction. The Prophet 'Isa, son of Maryam, upon whom peace, called the Jews back to the Law that had been revealed to Musa, upon whom peace, and especially to stop the evil of riba. Riba is not "excessive interest". It is any interest. It is also any financial transaction with an imbalance in it – making money purely out of money – with an imbalance either in quantity or time. This of course means moneylending. But it includes creating money out of nothing and ascribing real value to valueless things, like numbers and balances, which are measures and not things. To ascribe value to something inherently non-existent is to purport to create value out of nothing, and that is forbidden as riba. If it is not stopped, it is the death of a society, for when man creates unnaturally, he has to destroy unnaturally.

The Prophet 'Isa – Jesus – may Allah give him peace and may Allah make his Prophethood known, smashed the tables of the practitioners of this unnatural creation – those who gave intrinsic value to measurements, including the measure of time. The word 'bank' derives from the Greek for 'table'. He turned the tables with a violence which makes Muslims proud of him and love him, may Allah give him peace, because he stood up to, and saved his people from, the foremost evil of his time, which is the foremost evil of our time. But only the Muslims now have the means to repeat this deed.

Violence will not overthrow the modern banks, because real wealth no longer resides in the buildings. Not even the tokens of its measurement reside there; what they now tell us is money is but numerical data. Yet the banks are still the tables that need to be turned. And the bankers are the high priests who must be stood up to.

Islam has not been properly shown to the people of our time. At most, people might have heard that committed Muslims pray five times a day and try to avoid interest. To avoid interest now is irrelevant. The issue is much deeper. What the Muslims have to offer is much greater, much more awe-inspiring than "ethical banking".

Islam, when practised, with correct Zakat, is the end of

banking. And the end of non-specie currency.

This could happen quickly or it could happen slowly. While their practices go on, so will their vast injustices and inequalities of wealth, their outsourced torture, their destruction of the planet, their poisoning of the seas and soil, their psychological oppression, their deranged social and financial experiments, their clinch of mankind in statistical structures – all of which are the harvest of that practice of riba and the outcome of going against nature, because allowing the principle and practice of riba brings on an environment in which all these things can and will be done, but without which, they will not be done.

Muslims, therefore, must tell their fellow human creatures about the One to Whom they submit, and they must tell them that He has forbidden riba. And their fellow human creatures must respond.

We have put Allah
and His Messenger First

Allah the Exalted says in His Noble Book:

$$وَمَنْ يُطِعِ ٱللَّهَ وَٱلرَّسُولَ$$
$$فَأُوْلَٰٓئِكَ مَعَ ٱلَّذِينَ أَنْعَمَ ٱللَّهُ عَلَيْهِم$$
$$مِّنَ ٱلنَّبِيِّۦنَ وَٱلصِّدِّيقِينَ وَٱلشُّهَدَآءِ وَٱلصَّٰلِحِينَ$$
$$وَحَسُنَ أُوْلَٰٓئِكَ رَفِيقًا ۝$$

Whoever obeys Allah and the Messenger
will be with those whom Allah has blessed:
the Prophets and the truthful,
the martyrs and the salihun.
What excellent company such people are!

As Muslims, we have already put Allah and his Messenger first.

Abdullah ibn Hisham reported: "We were with the Messenger of Allah, peace and blessings be upon him, and he was holding the hand of 'Umar ibn al-Khattab. 'Umar said to him, 'O Messenger of Allah,

لَأَنْتَ أَحَبُّ إِلَيَّ مِنْ كُلِّ شَيْءٍ إِلَّا نَفْسِي

you are more beloved to me than everything but myself.'

The Prophet said,

لَا وَالَّذِي نَفْسِي بِيَدِهِ
حَتَّى أَكُونَ أَحَبَّ إِلَيْكَ مِنْ نَفْسِكَ

This is often translated as:

'No, by the One in Whose hand is my self, not until I am actually more beloved to you than yourself.' In which case he, sallallahu 'alayhi wa sallam, was saying to 'Umar, radiallahu 'anhu, that he still had a step to take.

But because "hataa" can also mean "it is that" as well as "until", the statement can equally mean:

'No, by the one in whose hand is my soul, I am actually more beloved to you than yourself.'

To which 'Umar said,

$$\text{فَإِنَّهُ الآنَ وَاللهِ لَأَنْتَ أَحَبُّ إِلَيَّ مِنْ تَفْسِي}$$

'Now I have it: by Allah, you are more beloved to me than myself.'"

'Fa' implies immediacy. In this understanding, 'Umar did not change and become something he was not before. He realised what his condition already was, whereas before it had been hidden from him.

The Prophet said,

$$\text{الآنَ يَا عُمَر}$$

"Now you have it, O 'Umar!"

The Messenger of Allah, may Allah bless him and grant him peace, was telling 'Umar about something he already had. 'Umar already did love him more than himself, but did not realise it. The Messenger of Allah corrected him and said, "No, you actually love me more than you love yourself." And 'Umar confirmed this.

This exchange was transmitted to us as Sahih in the collection of Bukhari, and is universally known. In other words, its import is for us, and its meaning is for us. It is our own realisation that is being indicated.

We need not climb to a rarefied height of purity and

piety at which we are finally the perfect Muslims. We *are* Muslims. We have already been taken into the circle of Allah's love.

We already put Allah and His Messenger first by the acts of prayer, fasting, Zakat and Hajj, none of which can happen unless we put aside other things.

We must realise who we are and who Allah has already made us.

This will not lead us to a different, Islamic kind of life, into robes or onto a minbar, or into a position of Islamic renown or scholarship.

It will lead us to intimacy with Allah in our everyday lives right here and now in whatever land and in whatever culture we are in. It will lead us to familiarity with His Messenger, sallallahu 'alayhi wa sallam, and relief from fear and sorrow, as Allah promises:

$$\text{فَمَن تَبِعَ هُدَايَ فَلَاخَوْفٌ عَلَيْهِمْ وَلَاهُمْ يَحْزَنُونَ ﴿٣٨﴾}$$

Those who follow My guidance
will feel no fear and will know no sorrow.

So we are building on something that is already there We build on it by hearing Allah's guidance. Surat al-Ankabut:

اتْلُ مَآ أُوحِىَ إِلَيْكَ مِنَ ٱلْكِتَبِ
وَأَقِمِ ٱلصَّلَوٰةَ إِنَّ ٱلصَّلَوٰةَ تَنْهَىٰ عَنِ ٱلْفَحْشَآءِ وَٱلْمُنكَرِ
وَلَذِكْرُ ٱللَّهِ أَكْبَرُ وَٱللَّهُ يَعْلَمُ مَا تَصْنَعُونَ ۝

Recite what has been revealed to you of the Book
and establish prayer.
Prayer precludes indecency and wrongdoing.
And remembrance of Allah is greater still.
Allah knows what you do.

This famous ayat shows us three things. Firstly, the
Qur'an is for reciting. For those who know it all, it
means to recite it all. But for others it means recite what
you know of the Book – *maa uhiya ilayk*, what has been
revealed to you, because what is commanded of the
Messenger, sallallahu 'alayhi wa sallam, is commanded
of the Believers, provided it is not specific to him.

Establish prayer: 'aqama' is to set up, which means we
set up the prayer in our lives by giving it a place in our
houses and at work, thinking of it in advance, being
in wudu, and steering away from situations in which it
would be difficult or impossible for us.

With this in place, major indecency becomes an almost
automatic impossibility, which is how prayer precludes
indecency and wrongdoing.

21

But remembrance of Allah is greater still.

Because remembrance of Allah – the moment of realisation – is the source of right action.

'Dhikrullah' means saying the name of Allah repeatedly. But it also means the act of remembering Him, the inner event of Him coming to consciousness. It is being occupied by thoughts of Him, subhanahu wa ta'ala, and being preoccupied by Him. And being taken over by awareness of Him.

This precludes being preoccupied by something else. The prayer trains the believer to move from his own preoccupations to being occupied with His Lord.

Anas ibn Malik narrated that the Messenger of Allah said, "There are three things that when they are in a person, he finds the sweetness of Iman: that he loves Allah and His Messenger more than anything else, that he loves his fellow man only for the sake of Allah, and that he hates to fall back into kufr as much as he would hate to be thrown into the Fire."

Once we realise that we love Allah and His Messenger more than anything else – and that this is not some unreachable station of the pious – we realise that we *do* love our fellow men for the sake of Allah.

* * *

Love of Allah and His Messenger unlocks a love of creation that is sweet.

Taking on the practice of Islam unblocks and activates an appreciation of one's own culture, homeland and family. This is why it is essential to distinguish Islam from culture. The degraded cultural practices of tribalism and marriage exclusively within the clan are not from Islam. It is *not* always preferable to marry within the tribe or race, especially if that tribe or race has become genetically precarious and socially isolated by too many close marriages.

When parents imprison their children psychologically under the pretext of Allah's command to obey one's parents, it becomes obligatory to escape, because the Messenger of Allah has indicated that we must love him – that we do love him, sallallahu 'alayhi wa sallam, more than anything else, which includes our parents.

This does not mean we do not love our parents. On the contrary. The practices of Islam and the example of our Prophet foster appreciation and love of our parents as well as an appreciation of and understanding of healthy culture, which is why Islam in any country will vastly strengthen all that is traditionally good in it, such as, in this country of England, courtesy, deep appreciation of nature, eloquence of expression, loyalty to legitimate leadership, steadfastness, genius of invention, courage and poetic expression.

The Muslim in England can appreciate the English hero Lord Nelson's steadfastness in suffering and in death, his famous care for his men, his charismatic personality and his genius for leadership that made him England's greatest naval hero and kept the Napoleonic menace off the island of Britain. We can also appreciate the English tradition of monarchy and its tradition of fair justice, even despite the condition at which these have sadly arrived.

But we are horrified by the perversion of the English qualities of the stiff upper lip and loyalty to King and Country which sent men into the trenches to be massacred in a meaningless war whose causes did not directly concern England. We are also horrified by wars which British, American and other people fight today, killing faraway humans for reasons unrelated to their own lives, under the pretext of national security. Meanwhile, more than twenty American servicemen commit suicide every day, which is a national security crisis in its own right.

But conversely, we appreciate England's history of worship and belief. Norfolk and Suffolk, for example, are said to have the greatest concentration of medieval churches anywhere in the world. Historians might say this is because of the riches of the wool industry and that affluent men competed to show off their wealth by building churches. This analysis stems from themselves. Believers know it is because the people here were people of belief – notwithstanding their Christian deviation – and Muslims also know that Allah has made the Muslims the natural inheritors of the mantle of belief in this land. This is neither a boast nor a choice. It is self-evident and it is something one may be part of or not be part of.

We must remember how important it is that Allah has made us Muslim. We must activate it in ourselves. The Messenger of Allah said of the person of Iman, "He must hate to fall back into kufr as much as he would hate to be thrown into the Fire." This means we defend ourselves from kufr. It means we are careful about what happens to us and how we associate with people. It does not mean we do not mingle or that we behave in a cultish, clandestine way. Rather it is the common sense and instinctive attitude of any healthy person who will keep away from and be on his guard against anyone who darkens his days.

An ayat of Qur'an which is a du'a the Muslims often make after the Khutba of Jumu'a is:

$$\text{رَبَّنَا لَا تُزِغْ قُلُوبَنَا بَعْدَ إِذْ هَدَيْتَنَا}$$

Our Lord, do not make our hearts deviate
after having guided us.

Part of the deviation of the heart, and the perversion of the nafs, is that it thinks it can work out what its own deviation is, whereas in fact its protection lies in being with people who brighten it and do not darken it.

Another du'a often repeated in the Jumu'a is:

نَعُوذُ بِالله مِن شُرورِ أنْفُسِنا
ومِنْ سَيِّئَاتِ أعْمَالِنا

We seek refuge in Allah from the badness of ourselves and from the wrongness of our actions.

What is not being asked for is that our selves become devoid of badness or that our actions all become good. The self is, in itself, bad, but Allah can cover it with His good. When our actions are good, it is because Allah has decreed it.

Preoccupation with His rightness means that we are not preoccupied with our own wrongness. Rather we are looking at Allah's rightness. This is called gratitude, which is inseparable from belief. The grateful person is looking at Allah's blessings.

We have put Allah and His Messenger first.

Allah the Exalted says,

$$وَإِذْ تَأَذَّنَ رَبُّكُمْ لَئِن شَكَرْتُمْ لَأَزِيدَنَّكُمْ وَلَئِن كَفَرْتُمْ إِنَّ عَذَابِي لَشَدِيدٌ ۝$$

And when your Lord announced:
"If you are grateful, I will certainly give you increase,
but if you are ungrateful, My punishment is severe."

By this we see not only that ingratitude and disbelief
are from the same linguistic root – k-f-r – but also that
we are promised increase if we are grateful.

So be grateful. Tell yourself and those around you
about the blessings in your life. Make it your habit to
see the good and not to see the bad.

Dividing up the Day

Allah the Exalted says in Surat al-A'raf:

وَإِذۡ أَخَذَ رَبُّكَ مِنۢ بَنِيٓ ءَادَمَ مِن ظُهُورِهِمۡ ذُرِّيَّتَهُمۡ وَأَشۡهَدَهُمۡ عَلَىٰٓ
أَنفُسِهِمۡ أَلَسۡتُ بِرَبِّكُمۡ قَالُوا۟ بَلَىٰ شَهِدۡنَآ أَن تَقُولُوا۟ يَوۡمَ ٱلۡقِيَٰمَةِ
إِنَّا كُنَّا عَنۡ هَٰذَا غَٰفِلِينَ ۝

When your Lord took out all their descendants
from the loins of the children of Adam
and made them testify against themselves
'Am I not your Lord?'
they said, 'We testify that indeed You are.'
Lest you say on the Day of Rising,
'We knew nothing of this.'

K-f-r means to cover. "Unbelief" is a weak translation, because it carries baggage left over from Christian dogma, and it implies a state in which the kuffar blithely go about their lives with this missing component called belief. They do lack belief, but it is not a missing component, it is the denial and covering-over of an existing component which they have and every human has, which is pre-existing, embedded knowledge of their reality.

> 'Am I not your Lord?'
> they said, 'We testify that indeed You are.'

Every person has testified to their slavehood and will admit it again once time comes to an end.

In the interim, they either realise their true status, or expend energy denying it to themselves. This is not some kind of internal struggle of good and evil. It is much more innately human than that. The word 'kafara' is to cover, conceal and hide the blessings which are outpouring. It is to deny that we are in a state of receiving all the time. The word for ingratitude is the same – k-f-r. It is to deny that one is being generously given to at every moment.

Gratitude, therefore, is close to Iman and something one nurtures, and we do so by talking to each other about the blessings we have received and the wonders in Allah's creation that we see about us. Even many of the kuffar practice gratitude, because they know that gratitude is healthy, although they do not know exactly why. When we do experience a setback or a tragedy, we search for blessings in it, even if an injured state may not be conducive to immediate gratitude.

By accepting Islam, one has already accepted gratitude as the basis of life. We do our prayers and would not consider missing them, whereas everything else is conditional. We may sometimes not eat, we may sometimes go without sleep, go without money, go without company or go without health, and we may even die, but we would not think about whether or not to pray. So we have already put our gratitude above all else. The framework is there. After that we embellish this pillar with extra words and actions of voluntary gratitude.

وَإِذْ تَأَذَّنَ رَبُّكُمْ لَئِن شَكَرْتُمْ لَأَزِيدَنَّكُمْ

And when your Lord announced:
"If you are grateful, I will certainly give you increase."

The Prophet said, "The prayer which Allah loves most is that of Da'ud. He used to sleep for half of the night, stand up for a third and sleep for a sixth.

This does not mean sacrificing hours of much-needed

sleep. It means that if you wake up early and do some 'ibada, then have a rest again afterwards before getting on with the day, Allah will be pleased with that and your life will change. How could your life not change if Allah becomes pleased with you?

Our prayers are a gift because they set up the structure for the night and the day, which is our fitra, the natural pattern of man.

Abu'l-'Abbas al-Mubarrad said that the Persian King Chosroes divided up his days as follows: a windy day for sleep; a cloudy day for hunting; a rainy day for drinking and play; and a sunny day for attending to people's needs. Ibn Khalawayh says, "Chosroes was not the most knowledgeable of them about the organisation of this world," and he quotes Allah's words, subhanahu wa ta'ala:

$$ يَعْلَمُونَ ظَٰهِرًا مِّنَ ٱلْحَيَوٰةِ ٱلدُّنْيَا وَهُمْ عَنِ ٱلْءَاخِرَةِ هُمْ غَٰفِلُونَ ۝ $$

They know an outward aspect of the life of the dunya
but are heedless of the Akhira.

Ibn Khalawayh goes on to say:

"Our Prophet divided his day into three parts: one part for Allah, one part for his family and one part for himself. Then he divided his own part between himself and his people. He asked the elite to help the common people, telling them to convey to him the needs of those unable to convey them themselves. If someone conveys the needs of someone who is unable to convey it, Allah will give him security on the Day of the Greatest Terror."

Ibn Khalawayh connects the division of the day with helping people, and helping people was described as conveying to the Prophet – the leader, in other words – the needs of those unable to convey it themselves.

Our Amirs and other people of natural authority fulfil this leadership role today in these outer matters and are conduits through whom the needs and concerns of the community pass. The Amir gets to hear about things, and can therefore make the best judgment.

Furthermore Allah, subhanahu wa ta'ala, says about dividing up the day:

وَجَعَلْنَا نَوْمَكُمْ سُبَاتًا ۝
وَجَعَلْنَا الَّيْلَ لِبَاسًا ۝ وَجَعَلْنَا النَّهَارَ مَعَاشًا ۝

We made your sleep a break.
We made the night a cloak.
We made the day for earning a living.

Sleep was referred to by the Messenger of Allah,

sallallahu 'alayhi wa sallam, as the "brother of death." And he said of himself, "My eyes sleep, but my heart does not sleep." This is also the state of some of the Awliya who have followed him: that their sleep is resting but not absolute unconsciousness. Rather their hearts are alive to the extent that they are not really put to sleep by the bodily shut-down which we call sleep. This is not a myth. It is a state bestowed on people. Then Allah says:

$$وَجَعَلْنَا ٱلَّيْلَ لِبَاسًا ۝$$

We made the night a cloak.

In other words, if sleep is abandoned in favour of worship, the night becomes a cloak to obscure the 'ibada of the grateful slave.

* * *

The Messenger of Allah, may Allah bless him and grant him peace, sent a delegate to Chosroes the King of Persia, who tore up his letter and had his kingdom torn up.

He, may Allah bless him and grant him peace, also sent delegates to Heraclius, Emperor of Byzantium, to the Negus, King of Abyssinia, to Harith Ghassani, governor of Syria, and Munzir ibn Sawa of Bahrain. He sent his Companions. He also sent numerous delegations to lesser tribes.

Reflect on how this Sunna translates to our situation here and now.

Kings do not rule us these days, nor is this a tribal society. Even politicians do not rule; they are the changing dramatis personae behind whom the directors issue orders. But all over society, there are people who hold authority at different levels and in different ways, whom we have Allah's permission to approach with wisdom, good measure and good adab.

There are also groups who, although without clear leadership, still associate strongly around commendable causes, and we may go to them too in a way which does not offend our own knowledge and integrity. It must be remembered that we have an authority and a knowledge which others do not have, even if we have little or no authority over people, and we may have less knowledge of this world.

I advise you to follow this Sunna of approaching leaders and groups, but not in isolation or on lone missions. Consult each other and involve each other. And accept the leadership of those of you who lead. Bring Islam to people in positions of authority.

And do not be afraid that speaking to important people will put your livelihood at risk. Allah says in Surat al-Waqi'a:

$$\text{أَفَبِهَٰذَا ٱلْحَدِيثِ أَنتُم مُّدْهِنُونَ ۞ وَتَجْعَلُونَ رِزْقَكُمْ أَنَّكُمْ تُكَذِّبُونَ ۞}$$

Do you nonetheless regard this discourse with scorn
and think your provision depends on
your denial of the truth?

While this is addressed to the deniers and not to the Muminun, we nevertheless take warning from it – we state what we know, without concern about our provision, and it is the truth of the One Who releases or withholds our provision.

This is like Allah's words about the deviators in Surat at-Tawba:

$$\text{ٱشْتَرَوْاْ بِـَٔايَٰتِ ٱللَّهِ ثَمَنًا قَلِيلًا}$$

They have sold Allah's Signs for a paltry price

– which is why we do not accept money for judgments or advice or the highest knowledge. Money may change hands for work in the dunya, and for trading, and even for teaching things like Arabic; and it is important to look after the people of knowledge well. But Allah says in Surat Ya Sin:

اِتَّبِعُوا۟ مَن لَّا يَسْئَلُكُمْ أَجْرًا وَهُم مُّهْتَدُونَ

Follow those who do not ask you for any wage
and who have received guidance.

So we do not follow those who insist on a wage for
guidance, because theirs is not guidance.

But this does not apply to leadership in this world. Abu
Bakr, may Allah be pleased with him, was an affluent
and successful trader, but at a certain point after he had
become Khalif, the Companions stopped him from
doing his trading and insisted he was paid from the
Bayt al-Mal, because his responsibilities of leading the
Muslims were too important, and exercising authority
in this world requires extra wealth, time and energy.

Beware of and be on guard against even the slightest
envy about other people's wealth and about the wealth
of leaders. To envy rich people is to hide one's own desire
for money by hating that others have it, a detestable
blemish of character and a sure route to misery. The
majority of the men of Uhud were wealthy. It is said
that when Abdarrahman ibn 'Awf died, rahimahullah,
they had to move his gold with shovels. The same is
said of Sa'ad ibn Abi Waqqas.

Wealth attaches to power. This is not morally wrong. It
is right and necessary. Were it not right, the Messenger

of Allah, may Allah bless him and grant him peace, would not have been granted a fifth of the spoils of war. Were it not right, the Zakat and the Jizya would not be decreed to go through the leader.

Wealth accrues at the power nexus but does not pile up there. It passes through. It does not stay and stagnate. The most legitimate reason for acquiring large amounts of wealth is to help the Muslims and exercise largesse. Instead of looking enviously and spitefully on wealthy Muslim leaders, we thank Allah that they are wealthy and counsel them and make du'a for them to use their wealth in acceptable ways, while being careful not to associate with them out of desire for money. And if it is clear they have come about it by corrupt means, then we turn away. But that does not mean believing the constant refrain in the media and books against wealthy leaders, which is regrettably echoed by some Muslims.

It is a detestable sickness of the age to vilify and denigrate wealthy people for being wealthy, and to resent those whom Allah has put above us in this world. True, the manner in which many of the wealthiest people have acquired wealth today is despicable beyond words – I mean the financiers and the speculators and the banking elite, who utilise the kind of transactions which are destroying the human race and the planet. We hate usurious, unjust behaviour and systems and must speak against them and establish alternatives until the end of time. But that is very different from a philosophy which claims that inherited wealth and the wealth of kings is bad per se. It is not. The origins of legitimate kingship and aristocracy can be noble, because lands and wealth can be awarded to those who perform great deeds of chivalry and heroism, serve the legitimate leader, and thereby help the greater good. For the leadership to promote such people and their families, and for those families to intermarry, is eminently good social practice. The fact that what now remains of aristocracy here in Europe is, as it were, severely reduced and sometimes nothing more than a carcass does not entitle us to hate it in itself.

Rather, we might well find the remains of the aristocracy to be some of the closest people to us; those who, through their connection to a noble past and their good breeding and manners, can quickly grasp the adab, service and generosity shown to us by our Prophet, may Allah bless him and grant him peace.

The aristocracy and royalty, therefore, remain some of the people whom we should hold in good opinion and approach with the message of Islam.

We must have a high expectation of Allah because Allah says in a Hadith Qudsi:

"My slave approaches Me with nothing more beloved to Me than what I have made obligatory upon him, and

My slave keeps drawing nearer to Me with voluntary actions until I love him. And when I love him, I am his hearing with which he hears, his sight with which he sees, his hand with which he grasps, and his foot with which he walks. If he asks me, I will give to him, and if he seeks refuge in Me, I will protect him."

This hadith was related by Imam Bukhari, Ahmad ibn Hanbal, al-Bayhaqi, and others with multiple contiguous chains of transmission, and is sound.

The voluntary actions most likely to bring this to you in this age are actions for the Deen and helping others whom you know. Constant giving to faraway tragedies and unknown people is itself a tragedy, because it makes us think that everything is alright where we are. It is not alright. The Muslims, and all people in your city and your country, are not alright and they need your help now.

Local Zakat

Allah the Exalted says in His Noble Book:

خُذْ مِنْ أَمْوَالِهِمْ صَدَقَةً
تُطَهِّرُهُمْ وَتُزَكِّيهِم بِهَا وَصَلِّ عَلَيْهِمْ
إِنَّ صَلَوٰتَكَ سَكَنٌ لَّهُمْ وَاللَّهُ سَمِيعٌ عَلِيمٌ ۝

Take Zakat from their wealth
to purify and cleanse them
and pray for them.
Your prayers bring relief to them.
Allah is All-Hearing, All-Knowing.

Here in the United Kingdom and in other non-Muslim countries in which Muslims live as minorities, Zakat should be taken by community leaders and distributed locally.

Estimates of how much Zakat is given in the UK range from 300 million to 1.5 billion pounds, but the figure could be even higher due to the private way it is given. Of this vast amount of money, an estimated 98% is sent abroad.

This reflects a situation in which the majority of Muslims in the UK originate in other countries, most of which are poorer and needier than this one. These Muslims feel an allegiance to and protectiveness towards the people in their countries of origin; indeed, many of them and their forefathers came here to provide financial security for their families back home, so the whole matter of being here is tied up with sending money abroad.

On top of that, we are bombarded with reports about the sorry state of other Muslims in places struck by catastrophe. So in fact, much of the Zakat goes to general disaster zones and not even to Muslims' countries of origin.

Furthermore, poverty in this country is not of the same stark kind as it is abroad. We seem to be held by the safety net of the welfare state and widespread employment. There is relatively little violence here, no famine, few natural disasters, and an excellent free healthcare system.

So why indeed should anyone give their Zakat locally?

The answer is that if we do not collect and give Zakat locally, we are doomed to remain a ghettoised, marginalised community resented for whatever wealth we may amass, with our Deen unrecognised by most of the indigenous people of this land. We will continue to be the favourite targets for people of hatred; unheard, ignored and looked down upon and considered a minority religion.

This is the forecast if Muslims do not bring themselves, and their Deen, fully into their adopted country and if they do not realise the sublime responsibility they carry.

Islam is the only intact, Divinely revealed life-pattern remaining.

Once this is grasped, it becomes imperative to offer it to whatever place we are in and to activate it among ourselves.

If we put in place the simple yet sublime orders we have received, we will not be able to escape their extraordinary consequences by the power and Lordship of Allah over every cause and its effects.

The Shahada, prayer, fasting and Hajj are all active here in Britain. But Zakat is short-circuited because of two things: lack of leadership and the channelling of funds to faraway places. Zakat requires a leader, just as the prayer in Jama'at requires an Imam. The leader is not necessarily an Islamic scholar, although the exception proves the rule. He is a trusted, notable man of influence and social standing, who knows his community and is esteemed by that community. He is someone who knows how to further the interests of his community and how to mobilise people and resources.

When Zakat is given to such an individual and he distributes it immediately and locally, it effects immediate change. It connects the wealthy of that community to its poor in an act of worship. It builds trust of the leader among the wealthy givers, and gratitude towards the leader and the Muslim community among the poor recipients. How can the poor Muslims struggling in this country be expected to look up to their leaders if those leaders are not seeing their situation and activating the Deen for their legitimate needs?

By withholding this benefit of the Deen from the poor in their own communities, leaders who advocate sending money abroad, and wealthy people who send it, become the very agency by which people are driven away from the Deen. The proof of this is in its opposite. The poor family who receives help from unknown wealthy neighbours, through their community or local leader, in obedience to the Command of Allah and the example of our Prophet, may Allah bless him and grant him peace, and in emulation of the rightly guided Muslims over the centuries – their hearts will incline towards the Deen, towards that leadership and towards their community.

The financial and social strengthening of local communities is an urgent need here, as the nation's political class become less and less deserving of respect and trust – if that is indeed possible – and as the state mechanisms by which wealth is taken and distributed nationally become more mechanised and invasive, while at the same time more estranging and intangible. Locally collected and distributed Zakat is the antidote to this and can help communities to coalesce, communities which will themselves be proof of the Deen of Allah, because the greatest proof of Allah, subhanahu wa ta'ala, is when people see the Muslims and the love they have for one another and the way they help each other. To see the Muslims together is above every argument.

I therefore beseech you to give your Zakat locally, to your Amir. If you do not have an Amir, find one, or appoint one. Or be one. From this action of local Zakat, we can hope for expansion, acclaim, success, protection, esteem and an increase in our Deen and in how we are seen and treated by others. And all success is by Allah.

* * *

Although poverty here is not like poverty in other countries, that is not a reason to send Zakat abroad, as the poor here are easily deserving of Zakat and vast numbers of Muslims are legal recipients, being either poor (fuqara) or indigent (miskeen). Muslims are the most economically disadvantaged religious group in the UK. Fifty percent of them live in poverty and almost half of them live in deprived areas.

The poverty of this society is of the kind where people are held in the semi-bondage of low level employment or welfare and given their basic needs. They live in the twilight zone. And if anything out of the ordinary happens to them, they are shipwrecked. Zakat, given locally by a local leader, embraces poorer Muslims with the beautiful ties of 'ibada, and gives meaning to the wealth of the wealthy.

In the time of 'Umar ibn Abdalaziz, some people collected Zakat in Ra'i, in present day Iran, and went with it to Kufa. The governor in Kufa said, "What is this? This is from Ra'i, it should stay there." It was sent back.

The first Hadith on Zakat in Bukhari says that the Messenger of Allah, sallallahu 'alayhi wa sallam, sent Muadh to the Yemen with the instruction to tell people about Islam. Zakat, he said, sallallahu 'alayhi wa sallam, was to be "taken from their rich and given back to their poor." In other words, from the rich of Yemen to the poor of Yemen.

In the Mudawwana, Malik is asked, "So the rule was to distribute in that place, unless it was too much, in which case it could then be transferred to the nearest place to it?" He replied, "Yes."

Ibn al-Qasim also said, "It has reached me that when 'Umar ibn al-Khattab sent Muadh ibn Jabal as a Zakat collector, he did not bring anything back with him. Malik said, 'The way for wealth to be distributed is for the governor to look first at the land wherein that wealth is and from where it has been collected. And if two lands are comparable, then he must show preference to the people of the local land and distribute it among the people there and not take any of it out of that land, unless some part of it remains left over, in which case he may transfer it to others.'"

It is true that he also gave governors the right to give it further afield to places where disaster had struck, but this was understood as an exception. Now, as with other exceptional dispensations in the Deen, the export of Zakat has become the norm and has changed the very nature of our religion.

* * *

What I have presented here rests on the conviction that we are on the right path and that all that he brought, sallallahu 'alayhi wa sallam, is true. It is obligatory to believe this of the Messenger and that he was entirely without fault and not subject to any of the inward shortcomings to which all other men are subject, with the exception of the other Prophets and Messengers, as I have said before.

Allah says, subhanahu wa ta'ala,

$$\text{وَإِنَّ لَكَ لَأَجْرًا غَيْرَ مَمْنُونٍ ۝ وَإِنَّكَ لَعَلَىٰ خُلُقٍ عَظِيمٍ ۝}$$

You will have a wage which never-fails.
Indeed you are truly vast in character.

This vastness of character includes not only his adab and acts of 'ibada and his peerless knowledge of his Lord, it means his actions directed at the wellbeing of his community, which were just as much a product of Divine Revelation and his sublime remembrance as everything else he did and said.

His actions, may Allah bless him and grant him peace, are the yardstick against which all actions are measured and they are the key to our success.

Qualities of Muhammad

– may Allah bless him and grant him peace

Look at the words of Qadi 'Iyad in his book *Ash-Shifa*:

He, sallallahu 'alayhi wa sallam, was neither excessively tall nor short. Neither pale nor excessively dark, nor was his hair curly or completely straight. He passed away with no more than twenty white hairs on his head. He had a proportionate body: broad shouldered, with his hair generally reaching his shoulders, although on other occasions it reached his earlobes or the middle of his ears. He would let his hair hang over his forehead, but later he began to part it; he would comb his hair and beard. He had a dense beard, a slight roundness to his face, and the pupils of his eyes were intensely black.

He had long eyelashes and a fine line of hair stretching from his chest to his navel like a twig. He walked with determination as if walking downhill.

This walk is a sign of intention, the opposite of which is doing things aimlessly. The people of Allah ask for Allah's forgiveness for doing anything at all without intention. He, sallallahu 'alayhi wa sallam, said, "Actions are by intention." You could say that all life's unfolding is a product of intention.

His face would shine as if it were the moon.

This is the light of Iman. It is the light of the prayer, which leaves a physical mark on the forehead and a spiritual mark on the physiognomy.

He had a pleasant voice.

Qadi 'Iyad also says that when he laughed, sallallahu 'alayhi wa sallam, it was a smile, and that he did not show the back of his throat or throw his head back. It was not raucous or uncontrolled laughter.

This pertains to self-control, like his words, sallallahu

'alayhi wa sallam, advising us to "suppress the yawn." It does not mean do not yawn. It means certain bodily functions are best contained. If you contain yawning and laughter, it illuminates the character. He, may Allah bless him and grant him peace, was also the most smiling of people.

> His cheekbones did not protrude and his mouth was wide. His stomach and chest were the same width. He had a lot of hair on his shoulders, forearms and upper chest. He had long upper arms, wide palms and thick fingers. His heels were not fleshy. In between his shoulders was the seal of prophethood like the button of a curtain canopy or a pigeon's egg.

This 'curtain button' is a simile particular to the Arabs. We could say, a pigeon's egg or a pebble on the beech.

> When he walked, it was as if the earth folded up for him; the Companions would exert themselves to keep up with him, while he would continue walking with ease.

> His favourite clothing was the tunic or qamis, white garments and hibarah, which was a type of red-striped upper garment.

This shows the permissibility of wearing different kinds

of clothing, including bright colours. He made things broad for us by not restricting himself to any particular colour or clothing. Islam is not about a particular style of clothing.

The Messenger of Allah's shirt sleeves would reach his wrist. On various occasions he wore a red-striped two-piece suit consisting of a waist-wrapper and a wrapper for the upper part of the body, a tight-sleeved and quilted double upper garment, a robe, a black turban whose two tails he let hang over his shoulders, and a wraparound made of animal hair. He would wear a ring, leather socks and sandals.

Just as he was perfect in spiritual strength, he was perfect in physical strength, as numerous reports demonstrate. It is narrated that Rukanah was the strongest man in the Quraysh, who, one day, happened to be alone with the Messenger of Allah on one of the mountain trails of Makkah, and so the Messenger of Allah said to him, "Rukanah, aren't you afraid of Allah and don't you accept what I am inviting you to?" Rukanah replied, "If I knew it were true, I would follow you." The Messenger of Allah said, "Tell me, if I defeat you in wrestling, will you accept that what I am saying is true?" He replied, "Yes," so he, sallallahu 'alayhi wa sallam, said, "Stand up then and let's wrestle." The Messenger of Allah grabbed him and threw him down because Rukanah lost control over himself. Then he said, "Do it again, Muhammad," so he threw him over again twice, to which he replied, "This is incredible, you're actually throwing me down."

Rukanah returned to his people and accepted Islam, and won the Prophet's companionship.

Qadi 'Iyad says in his *Ash-Shifa*:

> Allah purified him in spirit and body and kept him free from any faults and blemishes, and gave him wisdom and judgment. Allah used him to open eyes that were blind, hearts that were covered and ears that were deaf, and He made people believe in Him. Those to whom Allah had allotted a portion of the booty of happiness, honoured and helped him. Those for whom Allah had written wretchedness, rejected him and turned away from His signs.

He also says, may Allah reward him:

> If someone has been blessed with even
> one or two of the qualities of perfection
> and nobility – whether lineage, beauty,
> power, knowledge, forbearance, courage or
> generosity – he is considered noteworthy
> and people use him as an example. People's
> heart-felt esteem of these qualities makes
> people who have them honoured, long after
> they have died. So what then can be said of
> the worth of someone who possesses all of
> these qualities in such abundance that they
> cannot be counted or expressed in words? It
> would be impossible for him to have gained
> them either by graft or guile.

In other words, it was the way Allah had made our
Prophet, sallallahu 'alayhi wa sallam, which caused
people to believe in him and trust him. This includes
his innate attributes as well as the forms of his courtesy
and manners, all of which draw people close and make
them incline towards the one who has them.

Look at some of the other accounts of his qualities:

Anas said, "I have not smelled amber, musk or anything
more fragrant than the smell of the Messenger of Allah,
may Allah bless him and grant him peace."

In the hadith of 'Ikrima ibn 'Abdullah from Ibn 'Abbas, it says that the Prophet slept until he could be heard breathing deeply. Then he got up to pray without doing wudu'. 'Ikrima said, "That was because he, may Allah bless him and grant him peace, was protected."

Ahmad ibn Hanbal and others related that the Prophet could see eleven stars in the Pleiades. This, according to them, refers to the total which it is physically possible to see with the naked eye. Clear-sightedness is one of the special traits of the Prophets and one of their qualities.

Another of his qualities was that when he turned to face someone, he would turn to face them directly.

It is related that the Prophet said, "The kind of food which I prefer is that with many hands in it."

'Aisha said, "The Prophet, may Allah bless him and grant him peace, never filled his stomach completely. When he was with his family, he did not ask them for food nor desire it. If they fed it to him, he ate. He accepted whatever they served him and he drank whatever they gave him to drink."

* * *

The Messenger said, "I have left with you two matters which, if you hold firm to them you will never go astray

– the Book of Allah and the Sunna of His Prophet."

The Sunna is not the same as Hadith. Hadith are a record of the sayings of the Messenger of Allah, may Allah bless him and grant him peace. The Sunna is the behaviour of the Prophet, sallallahu 'alayhi wa sallam, and also, by consensus, his Companions. Sufyan ibn Uyaynah, one of the great scholars of Madinah and a contemporary of Malik, said,

"Hadith are a source of misguidance except for the fuqaha."

And Imam Malik himself said, "Many of these hadith are sources of misguidance. Indeed, there are hadith I have narrated that I wish I had never narrated and, for each one of which, I wish I had been whipped two times."

The Noble Hadith are particular to situations and require expertise. The Sunna is a very broad affair. For example, Shaykh 'Alawi al-Maliki says in his book on the Messenger of Allah, sallallahu 'alayhi wa sallam, that before he became the Messenger of Allah, he was at times a shepherd, and at other times he traded. Al-Sa'ib ibn Abi Sa'ib had a trade partnership with him before Islam, sallallahu 'alayhi wa sallam, and on the Day of Conquest the Messenger of Allah said to him, "Welcome, my brother and business partner."

Shaykh 'Alawi al-Maliki, rahimahullah, also says that he, sallallahu 'alayhi wa sallam, would neither flatter nor argue in business. He conducted business for Khadijah and travelled to Syria for it, and returned with an immense amount of money.

All this shows the permissibility of different states of livelihood and wealth, and that all of them can be praiseworthy. These matters are also part of the Sunna, and if they are followed with that intention, then that is an act of obedience to Allah, who says in His Book:

$$\text{مَّنْ يُطِعِ الرَّسُولَ فَقَدْ اَطَاعَ اَللَّهَ}$$

Whoever obeys the Messenger has obeyed Allah.

There are countless places in which we are commanded and encouraged to emulate him, sallallahu 'alayhi wa sallam. From one point of view, it can be said that Islam is nothing other than emulating the Messenger of Allah, may Allah bless him and grant him peace. When we emulate him, even if it is just by plying our trade with that intention, Allah puts baraka in what we do.

Know that Allah is aware of us entirely: when we remember and when we forget. We sleep and are subject to forgetfulness. His awareness is complete and absolute. Reflect on the light by which we see in this world. All physical light comes from the sun, either directly or indirectly, and it is the right amount for us. But were the sun to be too close to us, we would die, so reflect on the way creation is set up perfectly with no flaws, and the way it is saturated with metaphors and signs that indicate Him, subhanahu wa ta'ala.

Allah says in his Noble Book:

مَّا تَرَىٰ فِى خَلْقِ ٱلرَّحْمَٰنِ مِن تَفَٰوُتٍ

You will not find any flaw
in the creation of the All-Merciful.

This is the reason for some advice we were given when we went on Hajj. Our Shaykh, Shaykh 'Abdalqadir as-Sufi, may Allah have mercy on him and reward him, said, "Do not see dreadful things. See only good things." Do not see faults. One could be fully occupied with seeing the bad things people get up to on Hajj and the things that have been done around the Haramayn. But instead, live by the ayat: "You will not find any flaw in the creation of the All-Merciful."

Our Shaykh said on another occasion, "Hajj is your life." The advice therefore carries into our everyday lives. "Don't see dreadful things. See only good things." Ahmad Ibn 'Ajiba, may Allah have mercy on him, said,

"If only one could consider everyone a Wali of Allah." This is not excessive gullibility. It is a glance which seeks to have a good opinion. Allah says in a Hadith Qudsi, "I am in my slave's opinion of Me."

Prayer on the Prophet
and Intention

The Prophet, may Allah bless him and grant him peace, said, "There is no slave who prays for blessing on me but that the prayer issues quickly from his mouth, and there is no land or sea nor east nor west but that it passes by them and says, 'I am the prayer of such-and-such a person, which he prayed for Muhammad, the Chosen, the best of Allah's creation,' and there is nothing which does not bless him. From that prayer a bird is created for him which has 70,000 wings, and on every wing are 70,000 feathers, and in every feather are 70,000 faces, and in every face are 70,000 mouths, and in every mouth are 70,000 tongues, and every tongue glorifies Allah ta'ala in 70,000 languages, and Allah writes for him the reward of all of that."

Let us look at this.

Words have literal meanings and metaphorical meanings. Since the meaning of the hadith cannot be literal in the sense of physical, visible birds, feathers, faces and mouths as we normally understand them, we can permit ourselves to look at it in another way, noting that in the words of Allah and the words of His Messenger, sallallahu 'alayhi wa sallam, a metaphorical meaning may only be taken if the literal is not possible. And take note: we are not saying that the description is symbolic and the thing does not really exist. It exists, but in a way not immediately familiar to us.

When somebody prays for blessing on Sayyiduna Muhammad, sallallahu 'alayhi wa sallam, a process takes place:

He said, sallallahu 'alayhi wa sallam: "There is no land or sea nor east nor west but that it passes by them and says, 'I am the prayer of such-and-such a person, which he prayed for Muhammad, the Chosen, the best of Allah's creation.'"

In other words, the prayer on the Prophet, and in fact everything we utter, comes into contact with and affects everything near and far, in ways great and small.

This is easy to understand, since two neighbouring atoms, two neighbouring molecules, two neighbouring cells, any two neighbouring objects cannot remain unaffected by each other's actions. It is impossible for there to be absolute disconnection between created objects and events. When we say something, it affects everything, since words are meanings in the form of physical vibrations that issue from the mouth.

And the words of ours which are prayer on the Prophet, sallallahu 'alayhi wa sallam, carry a very particular quality onto our neighbouring objects and out into the world, and they establish a very particular kind of connection between the utterer and the world at large. He said, sallallahu 'alayhi wa sallam:

"and there is nothing which does not bless him."

Everything in creation blesses him, sallallahu 'alayhi wa sallam. Do we understand how exactly that works? If we do not, then our position is one of acceptance without knowing the mechanism, for while in matters of the outward, knowledge consists of investigation and discrimination, in matters of the unseen inward, knowledge consists of assent and submission to the trusted source.

Then he said, sallallahu 'alayhi wa sallam:

"From that prayer a bird is created for him (i.e. the

utterer) which has 70,000 wings, and on every wing are 70,000 feathers, and in every feather are 70,000 faces, and in every face are 70,000 mouths, and in every mouth are 70,000 tongues, and every tongue glorifies Allah ta'ala in 70,000 languages."

In Arabic and indeed English, a number such as 70,000 does not necessarily mean seven multiplied by ten to the power of four and not a single one more or less. It can mean an uncountable number or a quantity beyond the ability of the mind to encompass.

So this statement certainly refers to an amount which is beyond the visualising imagination.

And what of the birds with seventy thousand wings, each with seventy thousand feathers? Again, since birds of this kind are not known to us in the normal creation, we may understand what is being said by considering its metaphors.

Wing can mean many things. The expression "winged word" means a well-known phrase. It is neither a single word, nor does it have wings like those of a bird, nor does it fly in the normal sense, but it does fly in the sense that it has spread far and wide. And if we say, "he was waiting in the wings," that metaphoric usage has even come to have a different literal meaning, as in "either side of something."

The word "mouth" has many meanings. It is the place where words and meanings emerge. It can be the mouth of a river, or the mouth of a cave. It can also mean talkativeness and in its plural it can mean people who need providing for. And it can be the place where one thing merges or opens up to a broader thing. The same multiple meanings exist for "tongue" and "language".

So what this account means is that every time you say prayer on the Prophet, sallallahu 'alayhi wa sallam, there is an issuing-forth of something whose features and description, while not visible to the eye, are so myriad upon myriad that they are beyond the compass of our visual imagination. And these myriad things, inconceivable in number, precisely like the atomic and subatomic structures, they "yusubbihu" – they issue forth praise, they emanate an affirmation of the One Who has named Himself Allah, subhanahu wa ta'ala.

This is also what happens when Qur'an is recited, and when we make the Takbir al-Ihram to begin the prayer, when we give a gift, when we smile at somebody – this vast, atomic and subatomic process of the glorification of the cells, the molecules, the protons, the nuclei, the electrons, and the subdivisions as yet undiscovered – all of this situation is emanating, in its own particular mode of articulation, or language – beyond our limited human idea of language – a perpetual statement. All things affirm Him, subhanahu wa ta'ala, and He is elevated high above all ascription.

At the end of the hadith, he says, sallallahu 'alayhi wa sallam, "and Allah writes for him the reward of all of that." In other words, the effects on us of these good things we put on our tongues are too numerous to encompass and they go into our balance.

As Muslims, this knowledge and these practices are our inheritance. They are our toolkit. They are our medicine box. They are our first-aid kit. They are our vehicle. They are the boat in which one sails the seas of life.

* * *

The Rasul, sallallahu 'alayhi wa sallam, said:

إِنَّمَا الْأَعْمَالُ بِالنِّيَّاتِ

Actions are by intentions.

Allah ta'ala steers every particle of creation at every instant, and every event, by the agency of its intention. The seed intends to be a tree – not with a verbalised, human intention like ours, but by an intention indistinguishable from its design and meaning – and in its cells and molecules, a process begins to stir. When the foetus quickens and begins to move, it is because the spirit is blown into it. What is this blowing into the foetus of the Ruh? The foetus starts to move. This is the blowing of the Ruh into the foetus. Before that, it was just flesh. Now, it is flesh as a vehicle for something higher.

It is not necessary to be able to visualise this steering process. Indeed, illustration and depiction of Allah's unseen realities is disliked and even forbidden, precisely because pictures of them, drawn or painted using outward forms we are familiar with, like the murals of the Christians showing angels, are necessarily a misrepresentation and become a veil to proper understanding.

The baby's body, the vessel which will carry this spirit, moves at the spirit's command. The spirit says "I am" – "I want" – "I see" – "I hear" – and the limbs move and the eyes open and the ears hear, even while in the womb, because Allah has given the vessel the quality of moving by the command of the Ruh.

We are that. Each of us is a carriage for a spirit, and that carriage moves and acts by the spirit's command. And the seat of the spirit is the heart, from which intention issues forth.

Hajj is a meeting of intentions.

In two million believing people, an intention arises in the heart: to go to a place which has no material significance to them, to a place with which they have no family or business connections, in a country where most of them do not speak the language, spending what is for many the largest amount of money they will ever spend – all this they do with a singular intention that has nothing to do with the world of things, nothing to do with the world of wealth, nothing to do with the world of achievements, nothing to do with the world of family, nothing to do with the world of physical wellbeing, nothing to do with the world of reputation, nothing to do with the world at all.

It is an intention they make for Allah and in emulation of and obedience to His Messenger, sallallahu 'alayhi wa salam.

And from that intention, multiplied by the number of Hajjis, comes the blessed meeting at the Ka'ba, the Ancient House, where the Muslims revolve around and around, but do not enter inside. When you arrive at the vast crucible of the Haram, you hear a sound like a hive of a million bees, the hum of a million du'as, but what you notice in that great amphitheatre is the relative quiet. The peace of the Tawaf. The great, unspoken knowledge, a presence that will not fit into the containment of words. That is like the heart itself.

All this is by intention.

The Rasul, sallallahu 'alayhi wa sallam, said:

إِنَّمَا الْأَعْمَالُ بِالنِّيَّاتِ

Actions are by intentions.

Man is intention, given form. We are intended.

Allah the Exalted says:

وَمَا خَلَقْتُ الْجِنَّ وَالإِنسَ إِلَّا لِيَعْبُدُونِ

I only created jinn and man to worship Me.

Our cells are in constant worship of Him and praise of Him, merely by doing what they are created to do. Our molecules and the molecules of everything else are in praise of Him, merely by behaving as they can only behave.

The five prayers which we undertake to do are not really the beginning of worship. They are the completion of worship. By accepting them and embracing them, we tether our will to the reality of what we as organisms are already doing. Even the disobedient slave is in obedience to this, in that he is acting out what Allah has decreed: that some of his slaves will disobey Him, subhanahu wa ta'ala – and may Allah make us obedient slaves and may Allah protect us from anything that is contrary to the Shari'ah of Sayyiduna Muhammad, sallallahu 'alayhi wa sallam.

Here is the du'a of the great Shaykh al-Jazuli, rahima-hullah, in his Dala'il al-Khayrat, which is all prayer on the Prophet, sallallahu 'alayhi wa sallam:

اَللَّهُمَّ بِبَرَكَةِ ٱلصَّلَاةِ عَلَيْهِ. اِجْعَلْنَا بِٱلصَّلَاةِ عَلَيْهِ مِنَ ٱلْفَائِزِينَ. وَعَلَى حَوْضِهِ مِنَ ٱلْوَارِدِينَ ٱلشَّارِبِينَ. وَبِسُنَّتِهِ وَطَاعَتِهِ مِنَ ٱلْعَامِلِينَ. وَلَا تَحُلْ بَيْنَنَا وَبَيْنَهُ يَوْمَ ٱلْقِيَامَةِ يَا رَبَّ ٱلْعَالَمِينَ. وَٱغْفِرْ لَنَا وَلِوَالِدِينَا وَلِجَمِيعِ ٱلْمُسْلِمِينَ. وَٱلْحَمْدُ لِلَّهِ رَبِّ ٱلْعَالَمِينَ.

"O Allah, by the baraka of his blessing, make us among the victorious by the prayer on him, and among those who come to drink from his water-basin, and those who act by his Sunna and obey him, and do not place a barrier between us and him on the Day of Resurrection, O Lord of the worlds, and forgive us and our parents and all Muslims, and praise be to Allah, Lord of the worlds."

Hajj

Surat al-Hajj:

وَأَذِّن فِي ٱلنَّاسِ بِٱلْحَجِّ
يَأْتُوكَ رِجَالاً وَعَلَىٰ كُلِّ ضَامِرٍ يَأْتِينَ مِن كُلِّ فَجٍّ عَمِيقٍ
لِّيَشْهَدُواْ مَنَـٰفِعَ لَهُمْ

Announce the Hajj to mankind.
They will come to you on foot
and on every sort of lean animal,
coming by every distant road
so that they can be present at what will profit them

Each year, with the permission of Allah and by the invitation of Allah, may He be exalted, people from every country in the world form groups to perform the Hajj.

What is this invitation from Allah? Without it, nobody can go. With it, a person will overcome every obstacle to be there.

The invitation to Hajj comes through the heart of the Hajji. He realises it is time to go. He knows he is obliged. The call comes from the House of Allah, subhanahu wa ta'ala, and the Hajji responds. He has to go. And he wants to go.

The Hajji responds by making the intention. Above all, Hajj is intention. Yes, the means must be found, difficulties must be surmounted, the rites must be performed. But it is by intention that it begins and by intention that it is completed.

The invitation of Allah is that He, subhanahu wa ta'ala, gives the Muslim the intention in his heart. The Hajji renews it again and again, setting aside such objections that the nafs and shaytan may insinuate.

It is said that in earlier times, as many as a fifth of people would fail to return from Hajj. Banditry, disease and wild animals were common. The land journey was immensely long. It has become much easier for the modern Hajji, but he faces other obstacles like astronomical cost, lack of freedom from employment at home, extreme overcrowding in the Haramayn, unkind rules and bureaucracy, and the usurpation of hospitality by corporations.

But to the Hajji with a clear intention, all these become precisely the means by which the grain of his or her character is refined and knowledge is gained – the knowledge he needs for the time in which he lives.

Someone might ask, "How much does it cost?" While this is valid and nobody has to go who does not have the means, it might be better to ask oneself, "Do I really want to go? Do I sense an obligation which is not of me, but which proceeds from inside of me?" In an age of universal debt, vast numbers of people would never go unless they looked at it this way, since debt negates the obligation to go.

As he approaches Makkah, the Hajji enters Ihram. For men it is wearing two cloths and shoes with no stitching. But it is also a state of being which forbids grooming, quarrelling, killing even a fly, and wrongdoing. Like the fast, it is abstention.

He gets to Makkah and heads straight for the House of Allah, looking up at it only once he has arrived in the crucible of the Masjid al-Haram, the centre of the human situation, the hub of the great wheel of mankind.

His eyes see it at last and arrival fills his heart. Here, even in the prayer, he looks forward and up at the House itself. Then he heads for the Black Stone and, despite the crowds, kisses it, then circles the House seven times together with people from all over the world.

Then he moves to the Maqam al-Ibrahim, performs two raka'ts in the eye of the storm, takes a drink of Zamzam, and heads to the rocky mound of Marwa, from which he begins the Sa'y, hurrying to Safa and back to Marwa in imitation of Hajjar, who was left in the desert with her and Sayyiduna Ibrahim's child without provision and went from one mound to the other looking desperately for travellers who might have water for baby Ismail, just as we move fretfully from one place to another, one consideration to another, looking into the world for our provision and rescue, only to find it with us, just as she found Zamzam between the two hillocks. Zamzam is still flowing today and the experience of Sa'y is still there today, being repeated in an endless stream, awaiting our presence at it so that we can be shown something of our own lives and the human situation.

Then, if he is performing the Hajj Ifrad, which is the only variation the Prophet ever performed, he will remain in Ihram until the eighth day of Dhul-Hijr.

There is a dispensation to come out of Ihram after Sa'y and sacrifice an animal to make up for this shortcoming, in which case it is called Hajj Tamattu or Hajj Qiran. This, like many dispensations, has now become the norm, even though there is less need for it today than there was before air travel made it easy to arrive near to the time of Hajj.

The state of Ihram is savoured by the Ifradi Hajji in a way unlikely for others, because, like fasting, it is an experience of purification which builds up over the days. The body is neglected, but it turns out not to have needed all the attention it was getting. Later, on the Eid, although it is a relief to wash, shave and don clean clothes, he finds himself missing the purity of Ihram.

So the Hajji spends his days in Makkah doing tawaf and kissing the Black Stone to which Sayyiduna 'Umar said, "I know you are only a stone which can neither bring benefit nor harm. Had I not seen the Prophet kiss you, sallallahu 'alayhi wa sallam, I would not have kissed you."

We kiss it because he kissed it, sallallahu 'alayhi wa sallam, and the Muslims have always kissed it. And this is why we do all of the things we do as Muslims, notwithstanding the benefits and reasons that emerge from that obedience.

Our Hajji finds his way to the Multazam, right between the door of the Ka'ba and the Black Stone, and asks Allah for everything he wants for himself and others, because anything that is asked for there is granted. That is when he realises that although he came to fulfil his own obligation, he actually came for others, because by his du'a, Allah will give to them.

Then on the eighth of Dhul-Hijr, he and his party leave Makkah for Mina. I say with his party, because although every one of the now mandatory Hajj tour operators will send you with its party, it is preferable to travel if you can with the people you live and practice your Deen with, and to form a party with them.

He spends the night at Mina then sets off after Subh of the niinth of Dhul-Hijr for the plain of 'Arafa. If he does not get to 'Arafa before sunset, he has no Hajj. Hajj *is* 'Arafa. And when he arrives, he finds nothing there. There are no rites. There is nothing but two million other Hajjis, dressed in the cloths many of them will be buried in, gathered where Adam and Eve were reunited after their expulsion from the Garden, and where they recognised each other – ma'arafa. All he has to do when he gets there is stand.

The Messenger of Allah, may Allah bless him and grant him peace, said, "When the Day of 'Arafa comes, Allah descends to the lowest heaven and praises the people there to the angels, saying, "Look at My slaves who have come to Me dishevelled, dusty and crying out from every deep valley. I call you to witness that I have forgiven them." The angels object, saying, "But my Lord, this man has done such and such a thing and also that woman…" Allah, Who is great and glorious replies, "I have forgiven them."

Allah says in his Noble Book:

فَإِذَآ أَفَضْتُم
مِّنْ عَرَفَٰتٍ فَاذْكُرُوا اللَّهَ عِندَ الْمَشْعَرِ الْحَرَامِ
وَاذْكُرُوهُ كَمَا هَدَىٰكُمْ
وَإِن كُنتُم مِّن قَبْلِهِۦ لَمِنَ الضَّآلِّينَ ۝

When you pour down from 'Arafa,
remember Allah at the Sacred Landmark.
Remember Him because He has guided you,
even though before this you were astray.

When the sun sets on 'Arafa, the Hajji heads back towards Mina and stops in the narrowing of the valley at Muzdalifa, where he collects a number of pebbles and spends part or all of the night resting in the open. It is a difficult narrowness which must be passed through.

After Subh on the tenth of Dhul-Hijr, which is the Eid al-'Adha, he returns to Mina and hurries to the Jamarat to throw his stones at the biggest pillar, casting out shaytan with every throw and shouting that Allah is Greater.

Greater than himself. Greater than shaytan. Greater than anything that could trouble or concern him.

He then heads back to Makkah, shaves his head, and performs the Tawaf al-Ifada to complete the rites of Hajj. After that he comes out of Ihram, washes and grooms, and heads back to Mina to spend two or three more days, returning to the Jamarats on each of them to stone the shaytans again.

Mina, a vast tent city in the eponymous valley, has traditionally been the political meeting-place of the Muslims where Sultans, Amirs and other people of influence would convene to discuss affairs. Due to the vast numbers and logistics of the modern Hajj it has been seen as expedient to separate us into national camps, reflecting our situation in the wider world. But one senses there the immense, segregated potential of the world community of Muslims which, given favourable conditions, will gather again to become by far the leading force for good.

Upon leaving Mina, the Hajji performs a farewell Tawaf then follows the courtesy of a visit to the Prophet in Madinah, which it is preferable to do after Hajj and not before, since it is not obligatory. This is the place to assimilate the profound impact of the Hajj and recover from its exertions, rather than returning straight back home.

Madinah is the sweetness of the Rawda, greeting Sayyiduna Muhammad, sallallahu 'alayhi wa sallam, greeting Sayyiduna Abu Bakr and 'Umar, radiallahu anhumma, greeting the inhabitants of the graveyard of Baqi', visiting Uhud, and meeting the living Awliya who inhabit that blessed city.

Then our Hajji returns home, changed forever, like a child newly born as our Messenger told us, sallallahu 'alayhi wa sallam. He is keen to bring his experience to bear on his everyday life, yet apprehensive about losing what he has tasted. But return he must. After the purifying, devastating, illuminating experience of Hajj, it is necessary to return to the world. It is the Sunna of Allah to temper us like a sword, first in fire and then in water, then again in fire and in water, until our base metal is transformed to gleaming, keen steel which can cleave and will not break.

If you look for good you will see no end of good. If you look for bad you will see no end of bad. This is true on Hajj and it is true in all of life and it is true from the moment of making the intention. It is not a naïve pretence that all is well. It is consciously abnegating the habit of criticising people, things and circumstances and developing the habit of genuine high expectation.

In the Hadith Qudsi, Allah says, "I am in my slave's opinion of Me, so have a good opinion of Me."

Awqaf

عن أبي هريرة رضي الله عنه

أن رسول الله صلى الله عليه وسلم قال:

إِذَا مَاتَ ابْنُ آدَمَ انْقَطَعَ عَمَلُهُ إِلَّا مِنْ ثَلَاثٍ:

صَدَقَةٌ جَارِيَةٌ،

أَوْ عِلْمٌ يُنْتَفَعُ بِهِ،

أَوْ وَلَدٌ صَالِحٌ يَدْعُو لَهُ.

"Abu Hurayrah, may Allah be pleased with him, narrated that the Messenger of Allah, sallallahu 'alayhi wa sallam, said, 'When a man dies, his actions come to an end except for three things: sadaqa that goes on;

knowledge which is beneficial; and a right-acting son who prays for him.'"

When Sultan Yavuz Selim took over Damascus, he restored the grave of the Shaykh al-Akbar, Muhiyyuddin Ibn 'Arabi, and activated a waqf in the Wali's honour. It specified that a daily soup was to be served at his graveside to the poor. The waqf even stipulated the amount of meat in each bowl of soup for each recipient. Property was allocated to pay for this. The waqf still operates today, having gone on as a sadaqa ever since.

To make a waqf is to dedicate a property or an amount of wealth to the benefit of the Muslims, seeking the pleasure of Allah, glory be to Him, so that it goes on giving in perpetuity.

Property for this purpose must be free of obligation. It can be a possession which produces revenue like a house or a shop or a car park or a farm. The one making the waqf stipulates its conditions and is called the waqif.

The dedicated property must satisfy these conditions:

1. It must belong to the waqif.

2. It must not be obtained by loan.

3. It must be something that brings revenue.

The deed of trust of the waqf is called, in Osmanli

terminology – which we use because of their pre-eminence in awqaf – a waqfiyye. The waqif stipulates his conditions in the waqfiyye. The waqfiyye states:

1. The property, with lists of items.

2. How it is going to be administered.

3. How the revenue is going to be spent and who the beneficiaries are.

4. Who is going to administer the waqf.

5. Ratification by the presiding qadi.

The Messenger of Allah, may Allah bless him and grant him peace, made his date orchard in Madinah al-Munawwara into a waqf to assist in the protection of Islam. He made another in Fadak into a waqf for travellers. 'Umar ibn al-Khattab, may Allah be pleased with him, set up a waqf for war veterans and to assist slaves in buying their freedom.

This meant that certain social causes began to be taken care of in perpetuity, from the very first years of Islam onwards. It has been the practice of the Muslim community ever since.

Awqaf have existed wherever Muslim society has spread, taking care of the needs of people. They reached their height under the Osmanlis, who made innumerable properties into awqaf. The second ruler Orhan Gazi dedicated the Makaja sub-district with all its revenue for a zawiya in 1324. Zahids, the poor and travellers would benefit from that waqf, receiving meals and staying there without payment. The waqfiyye reads:

"Shujauddin Orhan, son of Fakhruddin Osman, has made all of Makaja sub-district into a waqf, khalisan mukhlisan li wajhillah, to please Allah."

He then designates the property, the manager and the beneficiaries, and ends by saying:

"If anyone disputes these conditions, his objection is not acceptable according to the rules laid down by the Prophet, may Allah bless him and grant him peace. Whoever interferes, the curse of Allah, jalla jalaluhu, and the curse of Rasulullah, may Allah bless him and grant him peace, will be upon him."

It is witnessed by his siblings, his son and others, and dated mid Rabiul-Awwal 724, or March 1324.

As the Osmanli Devlet spread, not only the rulers, but sadrazams, wazirs, beylerbeys, sanjakbeys and many well-off Muslims competed with one another in dedicating waqfs. The giver knew that as long as people benefited from his endowment, the recording of his good deeds would endure. Furthermore, the waqif thereby protected his dedicated belongings from being confiscated, since no-one could interfere with them. And he guaranteed a good income for his descendants, because he appointed them its managers, and among the stipulations of the waqfiyye is the manager's salary, all of which is legitimate. The revenue emanating from dedicated property, shops, houses, orchards, fields, and so on would be spent firstly on maintaining the waqf, on purchasing goods and materials, and on paying the manager and his assistants and other staff. One tenth of the crops from the Makaja sub-district went to the manager, and this was not a small amount.

During the Osmanli era, people established waqfs and dedicated properties for every need that could be imagined.

Waqfs for funding jami' mosques, other mosques, and musallas in the country to perform the 'Eid and Jumu'a prayers, schools, libraries, zawiyas, dergahs, fountains, *sebils,* cisterns, ponds, wells, lakes, the repairing of roads, caravanserais, hospitals, cemeteries in the vicinity of mosques and outside towns, meadows for weak cattle and sheep to graze. Waqfs for Makkah and Madinah, dedicated to support the poor of the two sacred cities, to aid stranded pilgrims and to serve water and drinks to the hajjis.

Waqfs for learned men to speak in the mosques, to teach tafsir, hadith, and fiqh, to recite the Sahih and the

Dala'il al-Khayrat in mosques and at the graves of the awliya, and as cash rewards to children who completed the reading of the Qur'an. Waqfs dedicated to reciting the Mawlid in mosques and zawiyas, for organising visits from mosques to the *Lihya-i Sa'adet* (the beard hairs of the Messenger of Allah, may Allah bless him and grant him peace, kept in Topkapi with other sacred relics), for spending on making and maintaining lighting in mosques, for weeding the grass that grows on the walls of mosques and zawiyyas. Waqfs dedicated to serving dates, olives and water to the Muslims in the mosques on the evenings of Ramadan and other holy days.

Waqfs dedicated to distributing food and money among the poor at certain times, especially during Ramadan and other special nights; waqfs for providing house utensils and brides' trousseaus to poor girls, for arranging funerals for the poor, for purchasing clothes for poor children and for widows on the 'Eids, amounts of money dedicated to purchasing domestic utensils such as glasses and earthen pitchers to replace those broken by children and servants, to protect them from reproach.

Waqfs to help wayfarers and to set slaves free.

Waqfs for having the Qur'an and other religious books written out, for purchasing them, for repairing and binding them.

For all of these, huge amounts of money, large areas of real estate, farms and servants were allocated and dedicated.

There were waqfs for hospitals, fortified inns, supplying water, repairs, wells, cleaning, ice on hot days, maintaining beehives and running establishments for the mentally ill. They dedicated waqfs for widows, for feeding birds in winter when they could not find anything under the snow, for providing nurses to look after the children of working women, for looking after poor and orphaned children, for their education, and for covering mucus on roads with ashes.

Waqifs would build nice looking places for birds on the walls of their mosques and other buildings. A certain Mürseli Aga dedicated a waqf in Ödemish, western Anatolia, to storks left behind by the migrating flock because of illness. He dedicated the revenue of his waqf to feed the birds on liver and lung and tripe. Another waqif dedicated the revenue of his waqf to the birds that came into the towns and cities in winter looking for something to eat.

Then there was the *sadaqa tasi*, a one and a half metre high stone or pillar with a flat or concave surface on top. People would put money on top of it as sadaqa. Then, after 'Isha when everyone went home, those who needed money would go and take it, saving their honour, without coming together, not knowing one another. Some of the *sadaqa tasi* had a lid or cover so that people could not see whether a person was putting money in or taking it out.

Many well-off Muslims built madrasahs and assigned waqfs to finance the running of schools and universities, and these were widespread. The Osmanli government did not pay a penny for education until the time of the Tanzimat (1839) which marked the beginning of Europeanisation.

The Osmanlis adopted the tradition of the caravanserai from the Seljuks, their predecessors. Caravanserais gave shelter to caravans and travellers on horse and camel. They were built on the most frequented highways at reasonable distances. A caravan could depart from one caravanserai in the morning and reach another at mid-afternoon, or certainly before sunset. There were separate rooms for guests, each having a fireplace, and there were store-rooms for foodstuffs, a kitchen, a stable for the guests' horses and camels, fodder and straw for the animals, a warehouse for commercial goods, a mosque, a tank attached to the mosque for wudu', a hamam, a shoemaker who repaired shoes for the travellers and made new shoes for poor travellers without payment, and a farrier.

Any traveller, whoever he may be, regardless of his

nation, race or creed, would be a guest of the waqif for three days without any payment. Even if he were rich, a traveller would not pay anything. All expenses belonged to the waqf.

The Osmanlis followed the Seljuks in the hospital tradition as well. The first hospital in the Osmanli era was built by Yildirim Bayezid (1389–1402) in Bursa.

At the hospital built in Istanbul by Fatih Sultan Mehmet in 1471 as part of his külliyye there were one chief doctor, one chief surgeon and about 200 other doctors, functionaries, servants and so on. The patients were served the meat of red-legged partridge and pheasant, and if that was not available, the meat of nightingale and sparrow, according to his waqfiyye. The mentally ill were treated using music.

Fatih's son Bayezid II dedicated 90 villages, many shops in Istanbul and Edirne, and some public baths as his waqf for his külliyye which he built between 1484 and 1488 at Edirne. Its hospital had one chief physician, two doctors, two surgeons, two eye doctors, one chemist, five hospital attendants, one barber, one washer of the dead, one secretary, one steward, one butler, two cooks, one porter — 21 staff in all. This hospital was designed for 50 patients. In the central building, the patients lay under silken quilts and the mentally ill listened to a chorus of ten musicians three days a week as narrated by the famous traveller Evliya Celebi. The chemist at the hospital also gave free medicine to the poor.

* * *

All this was financed by awqaf. A complete system of social welfare existed because of this simple device shown to us by the Messenger of Allah, sallallahu 'alayhi wa sallam, and propelled by the motor force of the charitable intention of the believers. From the actions of the Messenger of Allah came an effulgence of benefits so rich and beautiful that it looked after the needs of whole societies for centuries.

Consider the flow of money in such an arrangement:

The donor gives his property as a waqf, seeking Allah's pleasure, as a perpetual sadaqa. He receives a reward that goes on for as long as the waqf goes on. He feels ease in his heart, knowing he has left something behind that will benefit people and benefit him in the Unseen after his death.

Tenants and users of the donated property pay rent into the waqf trust, knowing they are paying towards the cause stated in the waqfiyye. How different that must be to paying rent to a landlord so he can pay his mortgage to bankers, the cancer of mankind.

The money is received into the waqf. After benefiting the manager and his family and providing employment for staff running the blessed waqf, the remainder goes to the cause itself, such as assisting the poor, maintaining roads or feeding travellers.

And this is set up in perpetuity. The property is the possession of Allah and cannot be alienated by the state.

In the Osmanli Devlet and at other times and places in Muslim history, most of the needs of society were taken care of this way. The state was not required for this purpose and was therefore smaller and less invasive. This is the radical political proposal of Islam. And it happened for hundreds of years.

We are not calling for bygone practices. We are calling for a pattern of giving which is part of a healthy society's natural state. It is the future in abeyance.

Osmanli awqaf drew to an effective end as the Muslims began to adopt humanist ways and state structures, and as the colonial powers, moneylenders and misguided, ignorant Muslims moved to possess the properties on which the awqaf were based.

The British government made the abolition of the waqf system a condition of its loans in 1860 following the Crimean War, stating that a) foreign (i.e. British) citizens should be granted the right to possess state owned lands under the same conditions as Ottoman subjects, and b) the waqf system should be abolished.

The Muslims had never seen themselves as belonging to a "state" in the modern sense. They were a commonwealth of believers, whose fitri patterns, even while shaped and moulded by the ups and down of history, rulers and geography, gave rise again and again to a pattern that was Muslim society.

When the state, itself an unislamic proposition, came gradually to be considered the permanent construct to be venerated, defended and fought for, and the vehicle to which to turn for succour and in which to trust for protection, so it arrogated to itself the right to control the welfare of all its citizens. This way of thinking rendered perpetual charitable institutions superfluous and created dependent citizens. As the Muslims began to adopt this outlook, so too did they turn their needful eyes to the state in search of help. This was only made possible by a rhetoric that claimed "progress" and degraded everything in the past as "outdated".

At the beginning of the 20th century, after the deposition of Abdulhamid II, Turkish banners began to be raised for the abolition of awqaf, banners calling for the appropriation of their assets "in the name of the

People", as if they had not been there for the people in the first place.

Care was now to be legislated and state-run, where before it had been a tradition of Prophetic origin.

* * *

For those who have felt frustrated by political processes – why feel frustrated, when such a vast model lies open to us to enact, starting afresh?

It requires no party, no Left or Right. It does not require legislation, voting, justification or legitimisation. It does not require debate. It does not require governmental approval since it is not illegal, nor indeed in this time of ours would it invite government disapproval.

The Prophetic waqf of Islam is the simple seed which lies in our hand to plant, and it is up to Muslims of influence and Muslims of means and Muslims with a voice and thinking Muslims, and most of all Muslims with heart, to plant it. Establish awqaf for the social needs of ourselves and all the people around us and for the generations to come.

Ayasofya

In July 2020, Jumu'a was held in the Ayasofya Mosque in Istanbul, at last putting right what had been a terrible blemish on Turkey and the World Muslim Community.

Ayasofya Mosque can be considered the world's most geopolitically important mosque, notwithstanding the primacy in the Deen of the Haramayn, and the blessed Masjid al-Aqsa being the site of the Night Journey and Mi'raj.

It is the primary mosque of Istanbul, a city of supreme geographical and historical significance. Straddling the straits that connect the Mediterranean to the Black Sea,

Istanbul bridges two continents and guards the gateway to the seaboards of Bulgaria, Georgia, Ukraine and southern Russia, as well as standing watch over traffic to and from the mighty Danube and Dnieper rivers. Viewed on a map, Istanbul is at a crossroads, linking East and West, North and South, water and land, old and new. It has been referred to as the centre of the world.

Prior to the arrival of Islam, it served as imperial capital to the Eastern Roman, Latin and Byzantine empires, and was instrumental in the advancement of Christianity until its conquest by the Muslims in 1453, after which it became their capital.

Built up on a uniquely defensible, hilly peninsula overlooking the Sea of Marmara and the Bosphorus, Istanbul is peerlessly beautiful and a place of immense baraka.

The main mosque of this special city is Ayasofya. Its current structure was built before Islam, under the Christian Byzantine Emperor Justinian, between 532 and 537 AD on earlier Christian and pre-Christian foundations. It was at the time the largest interior space in the world and remained the world's largest cathedral for almost a thousand years. It was the epitome of Byzantine architecture and the jewel of Christendom for a millennium.

The Messenger of Allah, sallallahu 'alayhi wa sallam, foretold the conquest of Istanbul and praised the commander and army of that conquest, for which reason it became a popular aspiration for many Muslim expeditions, starting just forty years after his death, sallallahu 'alayhi wa sallam. That first siege was attended by the Companion Abu Ayyub al-Ansari, rahimahullah, the standard-bearer of the Messenger of Allah, sallallahu 'alayhi wa sallam, who insisted on going even though he was very old. He died and was buried outside the walls of the city. His grave was rediscovered 800 years later on the orders of sultan Mehmet Fatih, and is now the site of an important complex which attracts Muslims from around the world.

The change of regime and the change of Deen in Istanbul in 1453 marked the end of Europe's Medieval period, the final end of the Crusades, the permanent establishment of Islam in eastern Europe and the end of the Byzantine Empire.

The victorious Mehmet Fatih, 21 years old, moved in procession to the great cathedral, by then neglected by the dying regime, and declared it a mosque, ensuring its renewal, continuation and elevation as a place of Divine worship. Until the construction of Sultanahmet Mosque over a century later, it was the largest mosque of Istanbul.

Mehmet inherited by conquest the vast personal possessions of the last Byzantine emperor. This included Ayasofya, which he declared a waqf for the benefit of the Muslims until the end of time, and he announced a curse on anyone who undid this.

Ayasofya remained a place where Allah was worshipped until 1935, when Turkey's new secular leader converted it into a museum. His new republican government, having abolished the Khalifate and declared open war on Islam, removed the carpets, uncovered the Christian mosaics and announced it as a building dedicated to bygone artefacts and cultures past – and then left it to gradually deteriorate again, a spectacular but sad tourist-magnet. By the 1990s, the roof was leaking and moisture was coming up from below.

The new, post-Khalifal Turkish leader had closed the great mosque and barred the way to worship of his Lord, who says in Qur'an:

$$ إِنَّ ٱلَّذِينَ كَفَرُواْ وَصَدُّواْ عَن سَبِيلِ ٱللَّهِ قَدْ ضَلُّواْ ضَلَٰلًا بَعِيدًا $$

Those who are kafir
and bar access to the Way of Allah
have gone very far astray.

Now, by the wisdom of Allah, this mighty edifice can again be used properly for worship of the Real.

The decision by the current Presidency to open it has provoked various responses. Some see it as a revival of Osmanli heritage. Some as a spiritual necessity. Some as a legal right. Some as a purely political move – just as Mehmet's transformation of it into a mosque is seen as purely political by people seeking to erase spiritual motives from historic actions. Of course, the actions then, as now, were spiritual *and* political. It is the unique prerogative of Islam to balance outward and inward motives, to combine the spiritual with the political. We do not despise politics in favour of spirituality, nor do we look down on spirituality from a worldly high ground. The Deen is balanced.

Motives aside, for Muslim visitors to Istanbul, this opening means we can now pray Jumu'a and indeed all our prayers in Ayasofya again, where before it was disallowed. This is a continuation of the work of the present regime, who have invested vast amounts of time and money in restoring sites of worship which before had been neglected. There are over three thousand mosques in Istanbul and they are nowadays many times fuller than they were twenty five years ago.

* * *

Ayasofya as a museum was a black phase, marking as it did the dominance of humanism and the abolition of worship in the foremost mosque of the natural capital of the Muslim world.

It symbolised Turkey's submission to humanist ideals, the nation's Muslim identity having been split in half by the personnel and events of the nineteenth and early twentieth centuries.

It is Allah, subhanahu wa ta'ala, who is the One who causes civilisations to rise and fall away.

As usual, much of the discussion of this event in Western media used terms such as Islamist, fundamentalist, reformist, traditionalist, revivalist, extremist, modernist and reductionist, all of which signal a desire to observe and treat Islam as a phenomenon to be analysed, relativised, and, ultimately, dissected.

The psychology and nomenclature of "isms" has emerged out of the abolition of Divine worship and the establishment of humanism as the dominant belief system, looking down arrogantly on religion. Religion has become a matter of personal choice and a subject of academic investigation. It is the same with "Islamic concepts". There are, as I have said before, no Islamic concepts. Concepts are conceived in the minds of men.

It is no wonder that the Patriarchs of the Eastern

Christian churches, the Pope of Rome and other Christian leaders expressed discomfort at Ayasofya being de-museumed, as it exposes their own submission to the museumification of religion.

Some Turkish Muslims have objected too, such as one Muslim author writing in the New York Times that the move is against what they call "Islam's pluralist instincts." They cite the practice of preserving churches in lands taken over by the early Muslims, coupled with lines of the Qur'an mentioning our affinity to Christians and respect for their places of worship. This is true, but it omits to mention the unequivocal superiority of Islam which is not only self-evident, but so central to our Deen that it requires a separate and longer discussion. And they omit the Dhimma, which taxed the Christians and Jews in return for the protection of Dar al-Islam, including a conditional protection of their places of worship against intentional destruction. They are not our equals. Allah the exalted says,

$$قُلْ هَلْ يَسْتَوِے الَّذِينَ يَعْلَمُونَ وَالَّذِينَ لَا يَعْلَمُونَ$$

Are they the same, those who know
and those who do not know?

The esoteric deviation which has attempted to turn Islam into yet another "ism" in which we are in cosy co-existence with our co-religionists, all of us brothers in a brotherhood of mankind, is of course the utter abrogation of Islam (and any other active religion) and the creation of an entirely new religion, whose ultimate purpose is to eliminate Divine worship as the only remaining threat to the criminal, unnatural, rapacious, usurious financial practices on which modern societies are based.

The idea that Ayasofya should have been left as a cathedral by Mehmet Fatih on the basis of leaving churches untouched is not correct. In actual fact, innumerable churches were left untouched by the Osmanlis. But this does not mean that in 1453, Christendom's biggest and most important cathedral, recently the centre of the Christian world but by then in decline, should have been left to continue operating. Mehmet was entirely justified in changing it into a mosque, which it remained for nearly five hundred years.

Conversely, innumerable mosques in Europe and elsewhere were turned into churches after the departure of the Muslims as the Osmanli Devlet shrunk in its final years. One scholar recently counted 329 Osmanli places of Muslim worship converted to churches in Ukraine, Crimea, Georgia, Armenia, Bosnia, Cyprus, Croatia, Kosovo, Macedonia, Moldova, Romania and Serbia. Greece stands out above them all, yet this was not mentioned by the Greeks as they railed against the reclaiming of Ayasofya.

Christians themselves built the original church starting in 325 AD on the site of a pagan temple, which they had no compunction in removing. And rightly so. They established worship of God there in place of something much less, and Mehmet purified that worship in a further upgrade, free of the Christian lie that Isa son of Maryam – upon him peace and may his Prophethood be made known – was the 'son of God'.

If it were as people say, and Christians were our allies in worship, then those Christians would be celebrating with us the release of that great building from the sterile, dead status of museumship which announces the humanist victory over all religions. They would be breathing a sigh of relief because a people who hold Sayyiduna 'Isa in high esteem are once again in charge. But that is not what is at issue. The Christians have succumbed to the esoteric deviation. They have embraced the religion of Tolérance, that Tolérance so absolute and so utterly intolerant of us.

We do not subscribe to their beliefs. We know that each of us, and society collectively, is on a Divinely ordained Destiny which nobody can forestall and nobody can bring forward. And that success lies in Prophetic legitimacy.

We ask Allah, the Great, to protect the leadership of Turkey and give them guidance, to give them renewal, and to give them mercy for the believers like the mercy of the Wali of Allah, the *Ulu Hakan*, Sultan Abdulhamid II. And we ask Allah to surround the leadership of Turkey with people of certainty. We ask Allah to protect them and to protect the Turkish Muslims, and the Kurdish Muslims, and the Albanian Muslims, and the Syrian Muslims, and the Iraqi Muslims, and the Bosnian Muslims and all the Muslims who constituted the great Osmanli Devlet. We ask Allah to save them and us from the curse of nationalism. And we ask Allah to send them His helpers in the Unseen and His helpers in the seen.

Marriage and Reward

Allah the Exalted says in His Noble Book:

$$\text{مِّنَ ٱلْمُؤْمِنِينَ رِجَالٌ صَدَقُوا۟ مَا عَـٰهَدُوا۟ ٱللَّهَ عَلَيْهِ ۖ فَمِنْهُم مَّن قَضَىٰ نَحْبَهُۥ وَمِنْهُم مَّن يَنتَظِرُ ۖ وَمَا بَدَّلُوا۟ تَبْدِيلًا ۩}$$

Among the Muminun
there are men who have been true
to the contract they made with Allah.
Some of them have fulfilled their pact by death
and some are still waiting to do so,
not having changed in any way at all.

Anas said: "My uncle Anas ibn al-Nadr – after whom I was named Anas – failed to take part in the Battle of Badr and was extremely pained about it. He said: "I was absent from the first battle fought by the Messenger of Allah, Allah bless him and give him peace. By Allah, if Allah, subhanahu wa ta'ala, enables me to take part in any future fighting, He will see what I will do!" At the Battle of Uhud, when the Muslims were exposed, he said: "O Allah, I exonerate myself from that which these idolaters have brought and seek Your pardon for what these (meaning the Muslims) have done." He then proceeded with sword in hand. On the way, he met Sa'd ibn Mu'adh and said to him: 'Sa'd, by Allah, I can smell the scent of the Garden by Uhud.' He fought the mushrikun until he was killed. We found him among the dead. He had suffered eighty-something wounds, ranging from a blow with the sword, to a stab with spear to a hit by an arrow. They mutilated him to the extent that we did not recognise him. It was his sister who identified him by his finger. This verse – i.e. from Surat al-Ahzab – was then revealed. We used to say: 'This verse was revealed about him and his fellow Muslims – i.e. who died fighting.'"

The ayat "and some are still waiting to do so, not having changed in any way at all," was revealed about Talhah ibn 'Ubaydullah. He remained firm around the Messenger of Allah, Allah bless him and give him peace, at the Battle of Uhud until his hand was badly injured. The Messenger of Allah, Allah bless him and give him peace, said then: "O Allah, decree the Garden for Talhah!" Sayyiduna 'Ali, karamallahu wajhah, said about Talhah: "That is a man about whom a verse from the Book of Allah ta'ala was revealed. Talhah is of those who have already paid their vows. He will face no reckoning regarding that which he will do in the future." Talhah ibn Yahya reported that one day the Prophet, Allah bless him and give him peace, passed by Talhah ibn 'Ubaydullah and said: "This one is of those who have already paid their vows."

Further on in Surat al-Ahzab, Allah the Exalted says there is forgiveness and an immense reward for:

$$\text{اِنَّ الْمُسْلِمِينَ وَالْمُسْلِمَاتِ وَالْمُؤْمِنِينَ وَالْمُؤْمِنَاتِ وَالْقَانِتِينَ وَالْقَانِتَاتِ وَالصَّادِقِينَ وَالصَّادِقَاتِ وَالصَّابِرِينَ وَالصَّابِرَاتِ وَالْخَاشِعِينَ وَالْخَاشِعَاتِ وَالْمُتَصَدِّقِينَ وَالْمُتَصَدِّقَاتِ وَالصَّائِمِينَ وَالصَّائِمَاتِ وَالْحَافِظِينَ فُرُوجَهُمْ وَالْحَافِظَاتِ وَالذَّاكِرِينَ اللَّهَ كَثِيرًا وَالذَّاكِرَاتِ أَعَدَّ اللَّهُ لَهُمْ مَغْفِرَةً وَأَجْرًا عَظِيمًا ۝}$$

Men and women who are Muslims,
men and women who are Muminun,

men and women who are obedient,
men and women who are truthful,
men and women who are steadfast,
men and women who are humble,
men and women who give sadaqa,
men and women who fast,
men and women who guard their private parts,
men and women who remember Allah much:
Allah has prepared forgiveness for them and an
immense reward.

In this blessed ayat, Allah the Exalted has given us a curriculum of study, application and actions by which He will reward us with immense benefit and a release from the heaviness of the world.

ٱلْمُسْلِمِينَ وَالْمُسْلِمَٰتِ

Men and women who are Muslims,

In other words – Islam is the entrance qualification for this course. The door is closed to others.

وَالْمُؤْمِنِينَ وَالْمُؤْمِنَٰتِ

men and women who are Muminun,

Men and women who believe and have Iman, which is from 'aman' – a sense and a knowing that everything will be alright. Islam without belief is nifaq – may Allah protect us from it. And a complete lack of confidence that things will be alright, as espoused by the suicides, is a departure from Iman.

وَالْقَٰنِتِينَ وَالْقَٰنِتَٰتِ

men and women who are obedient,

They are obedient to Allah and His Messenger, and to the people of authority among them. They are people who accept Muslim authority.

وَالصَّٰدِقِينَ وَالصَّٰدِقَٰتِ

men and women who are truthful,

The determination to eliminate lies in oneself, great and small, inward and outward, is the daily practice and exercise of the Mumin.

وَالصَّٰبِرِينَ وَالصَّٰبِرَٰتِ

men and women who are steadfast,

Trials will come and go. Allah the Exalted says:

الٓمٓ ۝ أَحَسِبَ ٱلنَّاسُ أَن يُتْرَكُوٓا۟ أَن يَقُولُوٓا۟ءَامَنَّا وَهُمْ لَا يُفْتَنُونَ ۝

Alif Lam Mim
Do people imagine that they will be left to say,
'We have Iman,' and will not be tested?

And:

فَٱصۡبِرۡ صَبۡرًا جَمِيلًا ۝

Therefore be patient
with a patience which is beautiful.

In Surat al-Ahzab, He, subhanahu wa ta'ala, continues:

وَٱلۡخَٰشِعِينَ وَٱلۡخَٰشِعَٰتِ

men and women who are humble,

وَٱلۡمُتَصَدِّقِينَ وَٱلۡمُتَصَدِّقَٰتِ

men and women who give sadaqa,

Sadaqa is a smile. Sadaqa is Zakat – although that is a
Sadaqa that has conditions. Sadaqa is helping others.
Sadaqa is inviting people to your house to eat. Sadaqa is
giving good advice in the right way.

وَٱلصَّٰٓئِمِينَ وَٱلصَّٰٓئِمَٰتِ

men and women who fast,

وَالْحَـٰفِظِينَ فُرُوجَهُمْ وَالْحَـٰفِظَـٰتِ

men and women who guard their private parts,

This means, as well as covering our private parts, we
do not wear clothing that gives others too close an idea
of our bodily form. Rather, we choose clothing that
leaves something to the imagination, and which allows
our encounters with each other to be about something
other than our bodies. Covering certain parts of our
bodies is not primarily about identifying ourselves as
Muslims, although it may do that. It is not primarily a
religious symbol. It is about dressing properly, which
allows for another kind of human interaction and helps
preserve intimate relations for the right place and the
right time.

وَالذَّاكِرِينَ ٱللَّهَ كَثِيرًا وَالذَّاكِرَٰتِ

men and women who remember Allah much:

This is the final and greatest module in the curriculum of
forgiveness and an immense reward. Men and women
who remember Allah much. They say, "Allah." Openly
and secretly. Day and night. Morning and afternoon.

أَعَدَّ ٱللَّهُ لَهُم مَّغْفِرَةً وَأَجْرًا عَظِيمًا ۝

111

Allah has prepared forgiveness for them
and an immense reward.

In all these ayats, Allah in his Wisdom, from Whom nothing is hidden and no possibilities, past or future, are unknown – has coupled men and women, and it is almost a prerequisite for this curriculum that one is married. Almost – the exception proves the rule. Shaykh Muhammad ibn al-Habib, rahimahullah, said that he did not take unmarried men seriously. Marriage, said the Messenger of Allah, sallallahu 'alayhi wa sallam, is half the Deen.

Inquisitive outsiders sometimes ask Muslims how they even get married, wondering how we manage to link up without the mingling and clubbing and drinking and trying each other out which they consider normal. The age at which people marry has risen steadily ever since this behaviour began to become the norm, and now it is normal to reach one's thirties and even forties, increasingly unsure and uncertain, anxiously on the threshold of something whose purpose is less and less clear and familiar.

Marriage, in Islam, is a contract. The couple agree, with at least two witnesses, to be married, they agree on a dowry, which should not be so costly as to burden the groom unnecessarily, and they write down that they are marrying. The dowry is handed over, and they may then have full relations. Before that, they may not.

That is what is essential for being married. And it is advisable not to add so much extra that it becomes burdensome, like the marriages seen both outside and inside the Muslim community, in which so much money is spent, and there is so much expectation, anxiety and competition, that one sees already the seeds of unhappiness and strife being sown.

But what comes before marriage is key.

First comes the matching. This can be arranged. It can be by the mediation of friends. It can be through encounter and recognition. It can be through the madness of falling in love. All these are valid pathways.

But what will safeguard the matching is that these encounters and negotiations are guided by the counsel of reliable companions and relations. Without the mirror of reflection, the passions are wont to make us see things in whatever way affirms them.

Marriage usually produces children, and caring for those children will be a major everyday activity of a marriage. How will a prospective spouse shape up as a parent? What kind of background do they come from? – because they are likely to replicate it for their children. What are they like genetically? These questions are almost taboo now, because of the aggressive brainwashing we are subject to, which says that none of it is allowed to matter, and even that such questions are the root of evil. But ask a breeder of pedigree horses about the lengths to which they go to study the ancestry, behaviour, soundness, character and upbringing of a prospective mate for their mare. Why, when human unions are so much more important and have so much more impact in the world than racehorse breeding, do we allow ourselves to be deprived of at least some reflection on these questions?

The Messenger of Allah, sallallahu 'alayhi wa sallam, said that there are four reasons to marry a woman: wealth, lineage, beauty, and Deen.

To this latter, Deen, he, sallallahu 'alayhi wa sallam, added in other Hadith the advice to marry women who are "Saliha" and "Mumina". Saliha is like Salih, which, in its root, means being in the right place at the right time. Mumina is, again, from 'aman', which means a state of confidence in Allah's protection. If a woman or indeed a man is overly anxious about provision, there will be trouble.

A Muslim woman may not marry a non-Muslim man under any circumstances whatsoever. If a non-Muslim couple are already married and the woman becomes Muslim, she gives him a fixed time to consider the Deen, and if he refuses, she leaves him and the marriage is over. To stay on in such an arrangement amounts to illegitimate relations.

A Muslim man may marry a woman who says she is Christian or Jew, as she is from the People of the Book, but not any other woman, because it is prohibited and there is nothing good to be had from such a union. And even marrying a Christian or Jewish woman, while allowed in a Muslim society where the likelihood is that she will become Muslim or at least that she will not overly influence the upbringing of the children, is unlikely to succeed in circumstances in which the Muslims are a minority and in which Christianity and Judaism are to a large degree merely nominal.

On the face of it, the man usually initiates things, but inwardly it may be the woman who chooses. Therefore, for the man who wishes to marry, he should look to himself and make himself worthy of the kind of woman he seeks. Yes, this means being well groomed and healthy, and having enough money, but above all it means doing worthwhile actions.

Once the marriage is concluded, we follow the advice of Shaykh Muhammad ibn al-Habib, who said, "The key to a happy marriage is having guests." Guests in the house dispel the illusions and shaytans about which couples needlessly fight.

Shaykh 'Abdalqadir as-Sufi, may Allah reward him and make his teachings known, advised us to establish the prayer in the home. If the man leads the women and children in prayer, things will be in place – by Allah – but if not, the one with the strongest nafs will rule – by the nafs – be it man, woman or child.

The contract of marriage obliges the man to feed, house and clothe the woman and children. It obliges her not to go against him or withhold sexual relations; nor indeed may he withhold them from her. The wisdom of this apparently unequal but perfectly balanced arrangement is immense. The man must feed, house and clothe the woman and children, and she must not go against him, including in sexual relations.

If a man delegates this job of feeding and clothing and housing to the state, then he cannot expect to have authority and he may find his advances refused.

This is why it is rarely wise for a man to marry unless he has some income. It does not mean having a lot, although it should be stated clearly that wealth does aid marriage.

But nothing aids it like agreement in Iman and the remembrance of Allah, may He be exalted, over everyday affairs.

Marriage as a practice is over in Western societies, as

it has ceased to have any practical relevance and has become purely symbolic. Only the Muslims still have a clear picture of what it really entails. Muslims marrying therefore have a responsibility not only to themselves and their future children. They are responsible to all the people around them and to society at large, as they are becoming the only examples of the natural union between man and woman.

Good Company

Allah the Exalted says in His Noble Book:

$$يَـٰٓأَيُّهَا ٱلَّذِينَ ءَامَنُوا۟ ٱتَّقُوا۟ ٱللَّهَ وَكُونُوا۟ مَعَ ٱلصَّـٰدِقِينَ$$

You who have Iman! Have taqwa of Allah
and be with the truly sincere.

This is an order from our Lord:

If you believe: "be with the truly sincere."

You have to be with the Sadiqun. And in this age of ours, keeping good company takes precedence over everything, even knowledge of the Deen and personal assiduity of practice. Every age has priorities. Imam

119

Malik, radiallahu 'anhu, said that if you live in a time of drunkenness, lean heavily on the laws prohibiting alcohol. If you live in a time of licentiousness, lean heavily on the laws of adultery. And in our time of endemic loneliness and isolation, we must lean heavily on the Sunna of keeping company.

In a Muslim society with strong Muslim leadership, as has existed at various times in the past and may still exist in tiny pockets today (although if so, they are truly well hidden), one would be surrounded by Muslims all the time and the dangers facing the human being would be different. Even today, on Hajj, you are released from the usual diligence about keeping company, because there are only Muslims there and everyone is at their best.

But here, now, in this land and other industrialised countries, keeping good company is so important, that were one to have only one piece of advice to give, it would be: keep the best company.

Good company is, firstly, Muslim company. This is not a statement of prejudice. The Muslims have knowledge others do not have. They are submitted to Allah and have accepted His Messenger.

Other people are either uninformed, misguided, undecided, or opposed, and Allah knows best.

Uninformed means they have not heard about Allah and His Messenger, may Allah bless him and guide him peace. May Allah inform them!

Misguided means they have some Divine guidance but there are wrong things in it, like the Christians. May Allah guide them!

Undecided means they know about Islam but have not yet taken the step. May Allah complete them!

Opposed means they know about it and have gone on the offensive. May Allah defeat them!

Among the Muslims, some are better company than others, and among the non-Muslims, some are better company than others.

Good company, in general, is people of good speech. People who avoid bad things. People of good manners. People of good character. People of good nature. People of good opinion. People who avoid gossip and idle talk. People who keep their promises. People who are generous. These kinds of thing apply to everyone, Muslim or not.

Among the Muslims, good company reminds us of Allah. Good company holds to the five prayers. Good company gathers people for the prayer. Good company is not anxious about provision. Good company praises Allah and ascribes power to Him when things go well and when things go badly. Good company sees Allah's hand in everything. Good company mentions His Name a lot. Good company makes du'a for us.

Remember the blessings Allah has given you. You are Muslim. You have responded to the One Who commands your destiny. Even if we slip up or are weak in our obligations, or we think we are not good enough, Allah has chosen us as Muslims despite that, and however great we may think our wrong actions are, His forgiveness is greater.

One of the great du'as we recite at the end of the prayer is:

اللهم مغفرتك أوسع من ذنوبي
ورحمتك أرجى عندي من عملي

O Allah, Your forgiveness is broader than my wrong actions and I place greater hope in Your mercy than in my actions.

As Muslims we have the opportunity and the tools to change ourselves in a way that others cannot. If you wish to improve your character, the Messenger of Allah exemplified perfect character and we are connected to him and know about him. And if we want deeper knowledge – knowledge of the realities upon which existence is based – then that too is open to us because nobody possessed greater knowledge of that than him, may Allah bless him and grant him peace. And if we want knowledge of how to better society, then that is open to us as because the Messenger of Allah changed society from something ignorant, prejudiced, unjust and based on wrong spiritual and intellectual foundations into the best society that has ever existed, one in which human transactions were directed in harmony with the creation process.

And if we want to take the path to the ultimate knowledge – direct knowledge of Allah – and there is no higher knowledge – then that too is open to us, because the Messenger of Allah was taken closer to Allah than any other person before or since, and he transmitted some of that knowledge to his Companions, face to face, and they transmitted that to their Companions, face to face, and so on, along chains of transmission that lead to this day.

There are people who have been granted this knowledge through direct transmission, and they are alive and in existence. The Messenger of Allah, may Allah bless him and grant him peace, said that there will always be forty people of the Station of Ibrahim. One must not think for a moment that the Awliya and people of direct witnessing are no longer alive.

If you wish to find such a person and set off on such

a journey, and your intention is sincere and strong, then you will find yourself travelling to him, and he will come to you, and you will meet, however far apart you may have been and however impossible it may have seemed. It is easy for Allah.

The nafs has strategies to sustain its idea of itself and who it is, and will try to sabotage this journey by saying excuses such as –

"That is not the kind of person I am."

"I am not good enough for those people."

"I am too good for those people."

"I want to meet the guide, but I don't like the people he is with."

"I would go, but maybe the guide is deviant and an innovator, so I had better stay away."

"I am not a good enough Muslim."

"My parents are opposed and I should always obey them."

"I can't afford it."

…and so on, in an endless stream of lies which the nafs tells you to make you fail and deny you the immense gifts that Allah places right in front of you.

Allah is Generous, and the greatest gifts lie with the people of knowledge and the people of divine gifts.

يَـٰٓأَيُّهَا ٱلَّذِينَ ءَامَنُواْ ٱتَّقُواْ ٱللَّهَ وَكُونُواْ مَعَ ٱلصَّـٰدِقِينَ

You who have Iman! Have taqwa of Allah
and be with the truly sincere.

* * *

The Muslims are a blessing for whatever country they find themselves in. We must recognise that and act out of that knowledge. We must fulfil our destiny to bring dynamic goodness and strength. We must work to find out what our contribution will be.

For some, it will be that their character changes people, and they will not even know it. One man I know was in London recently, walking home from a late shift, and he saw a Muslim praying by himself in a dark alleyway on a piece of cardboard in the rain. The sight of this changed him and strengthened him in his own prayer. The man in the alley was obeying his Lord and doing the prayer, and without knowing it, he helped someone else to worship their Lord.

However you got here, to this place, at this time, you must see Allah's hand in it. You must see Allah's hand in everything that unfolds for you. However much it seems like you were brought to where you are by your own decisions, the decisions of others, circumstances you could or could not change, your successes or failures, or good or bad things that were done by yourself or somebody else, you have to recognise that it was all by Allah and could not have been another way, even by an inch.

Ask yourself: what does Allah want of me here? Why did He bring me here? How can I serve Him here? How can I help people here? How can I bring goodness and dynamism and uprightness and strength to the situation I am in? How can I gain knowledge here and how can I use this opportunity of being here to become safer with Allah so that things go well, so that my family is well and others around me are well?

Even the most terrible and upsetting trials must be viewed in this way. This is not an 'affirmative life-view' or primitive positivism. We see it coming from Allah. It is responding to the way creation is set up. If you look for good, you will see good and you will get good – as far as the eye can see. If you look for bad you will see bad and get bad – as far as the eye can see.

The Modes of Man

Allah the Exalted says in His Noble Book:

إِنَّا لِلَّهِ وَإِنَّا إِلَيْهِ رَٰجِعُونَ ۝

We belong to Allah and to Him we will return.

Allah is our starting point. And He is our final destination.

A poet might describe a mountain as "the top of the world" of even "the peak of his own aspiration," whereas a geographer would speak about elevation above sea-level, geological formations, glacial erosion and soil types. Both are correct descriptions of the same phenomenon: "the mountain". But they are seen through different eyes. They use different modes of discussion.

Let us look at the modes in which we describe the unseen worlds, those layers of existence we cannot see with our physical eye, such as our feelings, our psychological states, the unseen processes of creation, the ways we affect one another – but most importantly, the realms of belief.

Allah, subhanahu wa ta'ala, describes the Qur'an as the Book that is for:

$$ اَلَّذِينَ يُؤْمِنُونَ بِالْغَيْبِ $$

those who have Iman in the Unseen.

And in the Hadith of Jibril, we are taught that Iman, belief, is belief in:

Allah, His Messengers, His Books, the Angels, the Last Day, the Decree – the good of it and the bad of it.

As Muslims in countries like this, we find ourselves surrounded by people who do not know about these things, and they hold totally different positions about the operating principles of the universe, including the way they themselves work as human creatures, and what will happen to them after they die, which can range from going to the worms, to not knowing, all the way to perpetual reincarnation.

The discussion of this matter is widely acknowledged as the ultimate question. It is as Allah says:

$$ عَمَّ يَتَسَآءَلُونَ ۝ عَنِ ٱلنَّبَإِ ٱلۡعَظِيمِ ۝ ٱلَّذِي هُمۡ فِيهِ مُخۡتَلِفُونَ ۝ $$

About what are they asking one another?
About the momentous news:
the thing about which they differ.

The news is what will happen to us in our ultimate destiny. The Muslims are the ones who have accepted the unadulterated Divine statement on this matter and who give the words of Allah precedence over whatever they themselves or others may at various times see, think or feel. They do this because of their Iman – a clarity of heart which, once established, takes sovereignty over but does not contradict other faculties such as the mind, emotions, rational conjecture, opinions, and the physical faculties. Once Iman is established in the heart, all of these other faculties are revealed to the heart as different modes in which we operate in and talk about the created world. But they are not fit for the purpose of contemplating the Unseen, let alone penetrating our ultimate destiny.

The faculty of the mind is used to harness benefit from situations, things and people, to negotiate the various circumstances of day-to-day living, and to plan human affairs.

Our emotions come into play especially in our interactions with each other, in our experience of life, like the weather in flux over every landscape, responding to things and events as affirming and negating voices, guiding us towards good and away from bad.

Our rational faculty is used to choose within the realm of conjecture and arrive at rational proofs and disproofs, so that we can understand, steer and replicate events for our benefit and the benefit of others.

Our physical faculties are our bodies operating in the tangible realm and enable us to fulfil our needs and enact our intentions and inclinations.

None of these is separate from the others. Nor are they located in different places or areas to the exclusion of the others. They are different modes of the same phenomenon: man. And each mode has its language.

The mode of the physical faculties is that we walk, talk, see, eat, speak, lift, reproduce, sleep and are creatures. It is the mode in which conventional Western medicine operates. To invade the realm of meaning in this mode would produce the idea that once the human organism is dead, there is nothing else.

The mode of the rational is that we use a particular

tendency of our minds to contemplate cause and effect: "You are wrong because of such-and-such." "This is like that because of this." "When this happens, that is the result." The mind is also the mode of contemplating physical and conceptual affairs, such as the patterns of how people organise themselves politically.

If it invades the realm of purpose, it produces statements such as "I think, therefore I am," which is like saying that thought is the summit of our existence – which, for people whose other faculties are stunted or cowed into submission to rationale, may well seem to be the case.

The emotional mode is what we feel about it all. Repelled, overjoyed, indifferent, we crave, we are shocked, we are even-keeled, we are refreshed. But if life's purpose is looked at through the emotions, we could say almost anything at any given time: "I can't bear to live," or "I live life the way I want," or "I'm a happy person," or, as the Dalai Lama pronounced with such stunning ignorance and insensitivity, "The purpose of life is to be happy." The emotions, if unguided, can also lead us to believe in whatever supposedly eternal scenario best fits our hopes and desires, rather than what is actually going on.

These modes – of which this is merely a fleeting sketch – collectively make up man, and they are indivisible. They overlap and merge. Whenever something happens, it will always elicit some shade of emotion, be seen within a rational enframing and produce a physical response in the body. All this happens as one intricate process which is man. Allah's steering of this process is called Rububiyya, or Lordship. He is Rabbil-'Alamin, the One Lord of all the different worlds.

Belief is different, in that all the other modes proceed from and are propelled by the heart, which is the seat of belief, but they cannot get to the core of the heart and its belief, because belief is not *of* them. Belief has its own language and its own terms and is beyond the sole remit of the mind, the physical body and the emotions. And when it is challenged by faculties which cannot reach it, it becomes as if it were not there at all. The oyster closes its shell.

When the heart is rusty, the other faculties appear to dominate. And they cannot encompass belief, so they reject it.

إِذَا تُتْلَىٰ عَلَيْهِ ءَايَٰتُنَا قَالَ أَسَٰطِيرُ ٱلْأَوَّلِينَ ۞ كَلَّا بَلْ رَانَ عَلَىٰ قُلُوبِهِم مَّا كَانُوا۟ يَكْسِبُونَ ۞

When Our Signs are recited to him, he says,
'Just myths and legends of the previous peoples.'
No indeed: rather what they have earned
has rusted up their hearts.

The Muslim knows that the landscape of belief consists of belief in Allah, His Messengers, His Books, the Angels, the Last Day, the Decree – the good of it and the bad of it.

This landscape is the landscape of the heart's looking on the salient matters of belief. They have a physical aspect, such as the humanness of the Messenger, Allah bless him and grant him peace, who is the vessel of Divine realities that make him Messenger and not just man. And the mus-haf, or copy of Qur'an, and its recited words on our tongue, which are our recital of the word of Allah, but are themselves not the Word.

The landscape of Iman is something we can think about with our minds, but the mind is singularly unable to either prove or disprove its existence. And the emotions may play across the landscape of Iman like weather patterns, and we may feel any number of ways about it. One person might hate the mention of the angels, one person might feel relieved and settled, another excited, another scared, another sceptical. True recognition, however, has nothing to do with emotion.

Emotions can trigger thoughts. Such is the example of a person who connects certain things with childhood experiences. When he encounters the same thing again, it is so tied up with an old emotional reaction that the feeling and his childhood response is triggered again.

Whole behaviour patterns can be perpetuated in this way.

But none of these thoughts or emotions reach the realities of the secrets of the Unseen.

Sometimes we encounter other languages that speak of the unseen worlds and strive towards matters that are the precinct of belief.

For instance, the science of physics speaks of matter as atomic and subatomic particles, and sees the universe as made up of them and governed by the laws by which they interact. Careful physicists, while advocating the usefulness of their science, will not exclude the possibility that other principles might be in operation, or that the laws agreed on may ultimately prove inaccurate or inappropriate, as they already have throughout history and continue to do so.

The now dominant Western medical science considers the body in a similar way, as a physical entity, admitting only relatively recently that it is somehow interlinked with the mental and emotional faculties, but generally rejecting or ignoring any notion that what the person believes actually affects the workings of the body, even while candidly accepting the 'placebo effect'. This error of theirs has produced in its opponents an enormous body of alternative theory, much of which is unfortunately reactive rather than standing on its own feet, beholden as it is to the dominant methodology of rational proof and disproof, an approach which, in real terms, is now possessed by Big Business and politics.

The science of psychology looks at the mental, emotional and behavioural workings of the human being and has its language of wellbeing, depression, mental health, psychoses, issues, historical baggage and neuroses.

Then there are modes in which people see themselves and the world which are almost like religions, such as yoga and tai chi which, in the forms they have come to us today, may or may not entail beliefs relating to meaning and purpose, but certainly bring descriptions of the Unseen.

For example, there is the ancient Chinese word, Qi, which refers to a life-force which is said to exist in everything and not be absent in anything. This Qi is sometimes intimately tied up with a way of looking at the whole of existence, and even gives rise to ways of life. And sometimes it is taken more of less on its own, as something which is there, or useful as a description, but no more than that.

The question of whether Qi exists or not, or whether subatomic particles ultimately exist, or whether childhood issues exist or are just a construct of man, is not the question here. The useful question is: are we using the right set of eyes for what we are concerned with in any given moment?

If we are fixing our car, it serves us to understand its mechanics. If we have an illness, it can certainly be wise to understand the body. If we have childhood issues, it can serve us to understand their origins. If we want to work out an organisational issue or achieve a technological solution, it helps to gather strong analytical minds.

But these sciences ought not to be consulted on matters of belief, because, unless they are subsumed beneath the certainty of Iman, they will fail to see matters we know about through transmission from Allah and His Messenger. And if they are asked, these sciences will attempt to rise above their station.

Conversely, the knowledge given to us by Allah and His Messenger can be universally applied, even to the most worldly matters. If a jinn has possessed a person, then a jinn has possessed a person. That is not to say the person is not suffering psychological symptoms or even psychotic episodes, and that there is no psychotic process at work involving chemical changes in the body. There may well be. The possession of the person and the chemical-psychotic process are one and the same event, but described in different ways.

When we say the angels accompany us when we travel in

the way of Allah, it is because angels are accompanying us. The ease and blessings of the journey could be explained in other ways, and there is nothing wrong with that per se, and it may be more appropriate if we are talking to people who are likely to associate angels with wrong constructs from their past conditioning.

When we say that Allah provides for us, this does not negate the agency of the means, when we are talking in the mode of means. I did a job. I got paid. They gave me the money. Of course they did.

These are the different worlds of which Allah, subhanahu wa ta'ala, is the Lord. The worlds are uncountably numerous. The Lord is One. To be able to move between the modes appropriately is a mark of sanity. The Messenger of Allah, may Allah bless him and grant him peace, always spoke in terms that people would accept and understand.

Being Alone
and the Story of Yusuf

Allah the Exalted says in His Noble Book:

$$\text{إِنْ هُوَ إِلَّا ذِكْرٌ لِّلْعَٰلَمِينَ ۝ لِمَن شَآءَ مِنكُمْ أَن يَسْتَقِيمَ ۝}$$

It is nothing but a Reminder to all the worlds,
to whomever among you wishes to go straight.

What is this going straight?

Going straight is looking to your Lord inwardly and
acting with wisdom outwardly.

Inwardly, it is bringing oneself to remembrance of our Lord. He, subhanahu wa ta'ala, is the Creator of actions and events, but He, subhanahu wa ta'ala, is not changed by actions or events.

Outwardly, it is helping the Muslims and all of mankind, and speaking out against and preventing the great crimes.

Between these inward and outward actions lies the prayer.

The straight path is neither disobeying someone in authority simply because we disagree with them or don't like authority, nor is it slavishly or neurotically obeying them. Obedience in the world may be done as an act of wisdom. Disobedience in the world may be done as an act of wisdom.

The straight path is neither pretending there is no cause for concern when there is, nor is it allowing oneself to be consumed by anxiety. As Muslims, we are mercifully spared from the anxiety that is the everyday state of many. But the completion of Ihsan is that we have concern for others – even, and especially, frightened and lonely people – as our Messenger had concern for them. Have sympathy with those driven to fear or anxiety, since we cannot know the circumstances of others and they may have legitimate cause for concern and may be naturally predisposed to anxiety, and furthermore they may be alone.

One of the great curses of this age is being alone.

Being alone allows us to keep company with the shaytan of perpetual thoughts.

Being with the Muslims allows us to bathe in the presence of mercy.

Being alone allows us to keep company with the shaytan of faraway voices.

Being with the Muslims allays the voice of anxiety.

Being alone makes us look jealously at the Jama'at and see fault.

Being with the Muslims makes us present with what is real.

Being alone allows the shadows of terror to grow long.

Being with the Muslims brightens our days.

Being alone allows us to ossify and become fixed in worldly configurations.

Being with the Muslims keeps us fluid and in change.

Being alone puts us under pressure.

Being with the Muslims is a sublime normality.

Institutional debt at interest is different from owing

money to people you know. Lending money to others is permitted. But making it a sadaqa is better.

This society we are in is increasing its debt exponentially using money that does not exist. Governments borrow vast amounts, but from whom? It was said the Titanic was unsinkable and we now scorn them for saying it. With the financial system we have, that is the boat we are on today.

We must tend to our core. What is our core? Our core is certainty. How do we tend to our certainty? By putting the prayer first and being with the Muslims. If you put Allah first, Allah, subhanahu wa ta'ala, will put you first.

Allah ta'ala says in Surat al-Baqara:

وَلَنَبْلُوَنَّكُم بِشَيْءٍ مِّنَ ٱلْخَوْفِ وَٱلْجُوعِ
وَنَقْصٍ مِّنَ ٱلْأَمْوَٰلِ وَٱلْأَنفُسِ وَٱلثَّمَرَٰتِ وَبَشِّرِ ٱلصَّٰبِرِينَ ۝
ٱلَّذِينَ إِذَآ أَصَٰبَتْهُم مُّصِيبَةٌ
قَالُوٓا۟ إِنَّا لِلَّهِ وَإِنَّآ إِلَيْهِ رَٰجِعُونَ ۝
أُو۟لَٰٓئِكَ عَلَيْهِمْ صَلَوَٰتٌ مِّن رَّبِّهِمْ وَرَحْمَةٌ
وَأُو۟لَٰٓئِكَ هُمُ ٱلْمُهْتَدُونَ ۝

We will test you with a certain amount
of fear and hunger

and loss of wealth and life and fruits.
But give good news to the steadfast:
Those who, when disaster strikes them, say,
'We belong to Allah and to Him we will return.'
Those are the people who will have
blessings and mercy from their Lord;
they are the ones who are guided.

The true disaster is to lose one's certainty that Allah is in charge of all affairs, and that the Messenger Muhammad, sallallahu 'alayhi wa sallam, is true in what he says. Allah says:

إِنَّهُۥ لَقَوْلُ رَسُولٍ كَرِيمٍ ۝
ذِے قُوَّةٍ عِندَ ذِے الْعَرْشِ مَكِينٍ ۝ مُّطَاعٍ ثَمَّ أَمِينٍ ۝
وَمَا صَاحِبُكُم بِمَجْنُونٍ ۝

Truly it is the speech of a noble Messenger,
possessing great strength,
securely placed with the Lord of the Throne,
obeyed there, trustworthy.
Your companion is not mad.

Allah, subhanahu wa ta'ala, addresses the Muslims in their moment of uncertainty: truly it is the speech of a noble Messenger – and your companion is not mad.

Which is why we choose to recite what we know of the Book and keep company with other people who love to be reminded, and we avoid indulging in excessive conversation about anything that makes us forget this reality, and we close the door on voices that confuse and obscure it.

* * *

Here is the story of Yusuf, 'alayhi salam, as related by Allah, subhanahu wa ta'ala, in His Book:

When Yusuf told his father, 'Father! I saw
eleven bright stars, and the sun and moon as well.
I saw them all prostrate in front of me.'
He said, 'My son, do not tell your brothers your dream
lest they devise some scheme to injure you.
Shaytan is a clear-cut enemy to man.
Accordingly your Lord will pick you out
and teach you the true meaning of events
and perfectly fulfil His blessing on you
as well as on the family of Ya'qub
as He fulfilled it perfectly before
upon your forebears, Ibrahim and Ishaq.
Most certainly your Lord is Knowing, Wise.'

In Yusuf and his brothers there are Signs

for anyone who wants to ask.
When they declared, 'Yusuf and his brother
are dearer to our father than we are
although we constitute a powerful group.
Our father is clearly making a mistake.
Kill Yusuf or expel him to some land
so that your father will look to you alone
and then you can be people who do right.'
One of them said, 'Do not take Yusuf's life,
but throw him to the bottom of the well,
so that some travellers may discover him,
if this is something that you have to do.'
They said, 'Our Father! What is wrong with you
that you refuse to trust us with Yusuf
when in truth we only wish him well?
Why don't you send him out with us tomorrow
so he can enjoy himself and play about?
All of us will make sure that he is safe.'
He said, 'It grieves me to let him go with you.
I fear a wolf might come and eat him up
while you are heedless, not attending him.'
They said, 'If a wolf does come and eat him up
when together we make up a powerful group,
in that case we would truly be in loss!'
But when, in fact, they did go out with him
and gathered all together and agreed
to put him at the bottom of the well,
We then revealed to him that: 'You will

inform them of this deed they perpetrate
at a time when they are totally unaware.'
That night they came back to their father in tears,
saying, 'Father, we went out to run a race
and left Yusuf together with our things
and then a wolf appeared and ate him up
but you are never going to believe us now,
even though we are really telling the truth.'
They then produced his shirt with false blood on it.
He said, 'It is merely that your lower selves
have suggested something to you which you did;
but beauty lies in showing steadfastness.
It is Allah alone who is my Help
in face of the event that you describe.'

Some travellers came that way and then dispatched
their water-drawer who let his bucket down.
He said, 'Good news for me, I've found a boy!'
They then hid him away among their goods.
Allah knew very well what they were doing.
They sold him for a pittance, a few small coins,
considering him to be of little worth.
The Egyptian who had bought him told his wife,
'Look after him with honour and respect.
It's possible he will be of use to us
or perhaps we might adopt him as a son.'
And thus We established Yusuf in the land
to teach him the true meaning of events.

Allah is in control of His affair.
However, most of mankind do not know.
And then when he became a full-grown man,
We gave him knowledge and right judgment too.
That is how We reward all doers of good.

Years pass and many extraordinary events befall Yusuf.
He is wrongly imprisoned, then released and made the
king's great advisor, saving the kingdom by his correct
reading of signs. Meanwhile, his father has turned blind
out of grief for losing him. Eventually the brothers are
brought into Yusuf's presence, without knowing who
he is. Allah says:

So when they came into his presence, they said,
'Your Eminence! Hardship has hit us and
our families. We bring scant merchandise,
but fill the measure for us generously.
Allah always rewards a generous giver.'
He said, 'Are you aware of what you did
to Yusuf and his brother in ignorance?'
They said, 'Are you Yusuf?' He said, 'I am
indeed Yusuf, and this here is my brother.
Allah has acted graciously to us.
As for those who fear Allah and are steadfast,
Allah does not allow to go to waste
the wage of any people who do good.'
They said, 'By Allah, Allah has favoured you

above us. Clearly we were in the wrong.'
He said, 'No blame at all will fall on you.
Today you have forgiveness from Allah.
He is the Most Merciful of the merciful.
Go with this shirt of mine and cast it on
my father's face and he will see again.
Then come to me with all your families.'

And when the caravan went on its way,
their father said, 'I can smell Yusuf's scent!
You probably think I have become senile.'
They said, 'By Allah! Your mind is still astray.'
But when the bringer of the good news came,
he cast it on his face and sight returned.
He said, 'Did I not say to you before,
I know things from Allah you do not know?'
They said, 'Our father, may we be forgiven
for all the many wrongs that we have done.
We were indeed greatly mistaken men.'
He said, 'I will ask my Lord to pardon you.
He is Ever-Forgiving, Most Merciful.'
Then when they entered into Yusuf's presence,
he drew his parents close to him and said,
'Enter Egypt safe and sound, if Allah wills.'
He raised his parents up onto the throne.
The others fell prostrate in front of him.
He said, 'My father, truly this is now
the interpretation of the dream I had.

My Lord has made it all come true; and He
was kind to me by letting me out of prison
and brought you from the desert when Shaytan
had caused dissent between me and my brothers.
My Lord is kind to anyone He wills.
He is indeed All-Knowing and All-Wise.
My Lord, You have granted power to me on earth
and taught me the true meaning of events.
Originator of the heavens and earth,
You are my Friend in this world and the Next.
So take me as a Muslim at my death
and join me to the people who are salihun.'

Islam in Britain

Allah, the Vast, the Great, tells us in the Qur'an:

$$\text{اِلَّذِينَ يَذْكُرُونَ اللَّهَ قِيَـٰمًا وَقُعُودًا وَعَلَىٰ جُنُوبِهِـمْ وَيَتَفَكَّرُونَ فِى خَلْقِ السَّمَـٰوَٰتِ وَالْأَرْضِ رَبَّنَا مَا خَلَقْتَ هَـٰذَا بَـٰطِلًا سُبْحَـٰنَكَ فَقِنَا عَذَابَ النَّارِ ۝}$$

Those who remember Allah,
standing, sitting and lying on their sides,
and reflect on the creation
of the heavens and the earth:
'Our Lord, You have not created this for nothing.

Glory be to You!
So safeguard us from the punishment of the Fire.

Think about and be appraised of how the Muslims come to be here on this island called Britain and in this country called England. Allah, subhanahu wa ta'ala, orders us to reflect. Let us survey our history very briefly.

In its prehistory, the island of Britain was populated by Celtic peoples. Then came the Romans, who utterly overwhelmed them. To the Celts they must have seemed unreachably modern, just as colonising empires seemed unreachably modern to conquered countries in more recent times. But a few hundred years later, the Romans left entirely, for reasons that had little to do with what was happening here. The southern half of the island of Britain was migrated into afterwards by a succession of Germanic tribes known now as Anglo-Saxons, who were ruled by kings in different regions. The northern half had its own people, with a history and language unique to themselves.

Then came waves of Scandinavians, who brought violent pillage, but who also settled and integrated and did not impose a Deen. What is now Normandy was also settled by them, and in time, in the working-out of political arrangements and by the impulse of expansion, men from there came to invade the south of Britain, led by William, the Norman – i.e. the Norseman, descendant of Vikings. He came with a new technology called castles and used them to conquer this land. Some of them still exist.

For quite a long time afterwards, French – not English or Anglo-Saxon – was the language of the ruling classes in what was quickly to become the unified realm of England. But because of political and personal decisions, social movement and plagues, French was gradually assimilated into and eclipsed by what was slowly becoming English.

There were no more successful military invasions of Britain after William. But there were some waves of immigrants, coming in search of better lives, and emigrants leaving for the same reason. There were incoming French, then Flemings and French Huguenots. Jews arrived with William to lend money, but were expelled under Henry I in 1290 because of the same practice, returning only under Cromwell. Other nationalities began to arrive from the British colonies in the 18th and 19th centuries, and most recently, in the break-up of the colonial world system during the Great European War of 1914 to 1945, larger numbers of people came here from the Indian Subcontinent, Africa, the Caribbean and other places. They, like previous arrivees on this island, gradually began to constitute part of what was considered British. Many of them were Muslim.

This island had been first a pagan then a Christian island. Prior to and after William there was a single Christian Church with the Pope as its acknowledged head, notwithstanding power struggles between kings and Popes.

These power struggles culminated in, but were not started by, Henry VIII, who broke from the Pope in the 1530s. The next hundred or more years saw the working-out of that schism, along with the transfer of land and wealth from the Church to the aristocracy, climaxing in the English Civil War and the execution of the politically impoverished King Charles I in 1649. That, and the death of his son Charles II, was the end of true, ruling monarchy on this island, and the beginning of a period of landed aristocratic rule through the instrument of Parliament. Kings and Queens, from then on, were subservient to the landed classes, even though some, periodically, showed the potential to rise out of this arrangement and assume autonomy, most recently Edward VIII, who was promptly replaced by the less threatening father of the present Queen, a substitution for which Edward's marital inclinations provided an ideal, if entirely hypocritical, narrative cover.

Relative stability was given to Britain by aristocratic rule until its utter destruction in the Great European War from 1914 to 1945, during and after which, rule passed over to a coalition between a professional political class and the owners of finance and industry, many of whom had and have no real allegiance to the people of the island. They were "international". Meanwhile, the ghost of monarchy lingered on.

Britain had persisted prior to this as a Christian place, meaning that many or most people attended Church, and nearly all people called themselves Christian. And, as witnessed in their writings and sayings, the majority actually believed in God and saw their destinies as guided by Providence.

But the aforementioned Great European War dealt the death blow to an already fatally weakened European Christianity, which was left afterwards as a hollow shell.

Now, as the last of the veterans of that War go to their graves, we are upon a period of passive agnosticism and ferocious atheism. By 2016, only 44 percent of the people on this island were even calling themselves Christian; 48 percent said they were of no religion; and 8 percent proclaimed other religions. Fifteen years earlier, 75 percent of British people had declared themselves Christian. This mass abandonment of Christianity, which has since continued apace, is in one sense cataclysmic since it signals a move away from some form of Divine worship, and we do not know where it will lead. But we do know it is part of Allah's plan.

By 2017, less than two million people were attending Church. The Muslims, meanwhile, were attending their mosques. Many of them also make their homes and workplaces into places of Divinely ordained prayer, just by laying down a prayer-mat, five times a day. And their population is growing around ten times faster than everyone else's.

Elements of Christian practice were maintained even until the twentieth century, but now there is little trace of doctrinal legitimacy; it has been subjugated to market forces and political correctness. Even heterosexual marriage, one of the last remaining enclaves of Christian authority, is now marginalised in Church media discourse.

And so, by the decree of Allah, most of the people among whom we now live, here and in other parts of this island, have, regardless of how they describe themselves, departed from any Divinely revealed practice.

But: many people – a great, silent, uncounted, unknown mass of people of this country, who are the ancestral product of this history of invasion and religious transition and decay, can be said to be waiting, in the historical and psychological sense. In that great, silent, uncounted, unknown mass, as we arrive in the present and find ourselves declaring the greatness of our Creator – there are people who will want to hear, because it is built into them to want to know, even if they do not know what it is they want to know.

What they want to know is: where are we ultimately from, where are we ultimately going, and to what purpose? What they want to hear is, for us, the normality of what we as Muslims bring to this island and what we do. We wash. We fast. We pray in ranks and in secret. We give Sadaqa and help people. We ask, we beg and we beseech our Creator – the Creator of ourselves and our actions – openly and secretly, in difficulty and in ease. We put Him first. And we recognise Prophetic legitimacy. We trust in our Prophet, Sayyiduna Muhammad, may Allah bless him and grant him peace. And we look to Allah and his Messenger in anything that besets us, personally and socially.

And we declare Allah's greatness.

None of this is in need of reform. The Muslims have guidance and a life-pattern. They are the guardians of Divine worship, the guardians of the possibility of civic health.

That waiting mass, the uncounted, secret many: they are waiting to know what we have, and it has not yet been given to them. Islam has not yet been properly shown to the people of our time.